COOL COOKING
COOKBOOK

COOL COOKING COOKBOOK

Cool Kitchen, Cool Cook—
Great Food!

Margaret Happel

Butterick Publishing

Art Direction: *Remo Cosentino*
Book Design: *Binnie Weissleder*
Photography: *Gordon E. Smith*

Pictured on the front cover: Mediterranean Salad (page 22).

The author and publisher thank the following for supplying props for use in the photography: Limited Additions, Inc., Shop 66, 1050 Second Avenue, New York, NY 10022; Manhattan Ad Hoc Housewares, 842 Lexington Avenue, New York, NY 10021; and Stephen Anson, Inc., 1058 First Avenue, New York, NY 10022.

Library of Congress Cataloging in Publication Data
Happel, Margaret.
    Cool cooking cookbook.
    (An EnergySaver cookbook from Butterick)
    Includes index.
    1. Cookery. 2. Energy conservation. I. Title. II. Series: EnergySaver cookbook from Butterick.
TX652.H363   641.7′9   79-24951
ISBN 0-88421-041-3

Manufactured and printed in the United States of America, published simultaneously in the USA and Canada.

CONTENTS

INTRODUCTION

As the cost of energy continues its upward spiral, here comes the *Cool Cooking Cookbook* to the rescue. Through four different approaches to food preparation, you'll discover the ease of making energy economies as you and your kitchen keep as cool as cucumber soup.

First, consider the possibilities for delicious dishes that require no cooking at all. With fresh fruits and vegetables in season, precooked meat and fish, and a few store-bought items, you can make all kinds of flavorful and filling soups, salads, desserts, even main courses—without touching a cooking appliance.

Certain foods must be cooked, however, so look into the second chapter of little-cook recipes. For some, just the merest hint of heat is required; other dishes bake for 10 minutes or so. But whichever little-cook recipe you prepare, the heat will never be on for more than 15 minutes.

With another approach to cool cooking, you can double your energy savings. When you barbecue outdoors, neither gas nor electricity is used—and your kitchen stays cool without expensive air conditioning. The recipes in the third chapter let you produce complete menus on the grill.

For a special way of saving energy—both your own and the kitchen's—choose a fast-food feast from the last chapter. On the way home, buy a bucket of ribs or a pizza as the focal point of your meal. Quickly reheat this main course with a dash of extra herbs or a tasty sauce, add a side dish or a salad, a simple dessert and your meal is ready to go.

Be sure to take advantage of all these energy-saving ideas for unhassled cooking. You'll find cool cooking means great food.

NO-COOK RECIPES

Simple dishes, elaborate ones, even entire meals can be prepared without turning on the oven or the stove-top burners. Fresh and crisp no-cook recipes have particular appetite appeal during the hot summer months, but they are delicious and refreshing through every month of the year.

What are the secrets of good, no-cook cooking? Here are a few tips you'll want to remember.

- Some of the best recipes feature only fresh vegetables and fruit. Look for produce that is of first-class quality; insist on the best, then chill it until you're ready to serve. Try Gingered Honeydew, Cucumber Salad or Fresh Fruit Salad with Fruit Dressing.
- Season carefully, perhaps a little heavier than usual since chilling often tends to lessen the intensity of the seasoning. If possible, taste again for seasoning after chilling.
- Have on hand a variety of sharp mustards, capers, salty anchovies, horseradish, hot peppers, relishes, pickles and spices like ginger and cinnamon to add interest and pungency to your no-cook recipes. The pure taste of fresh produce will be heightened and improved by the addition of imaginative extras.
- Very ripe vegetables and fruit such as tomatoes

and avocados can be pureed to a liquid state without any cooking at all. Thin the puree with chicken broth, cream, or oil and vinegar for a fast and flavorsome cold soup. Or follow the simple recipes here for Cold Spinach Soup, Cream of Avocado Soup and Gazpacho.

• Stock up on convenience foods that can be served without cooking, such as canned soups and broths, canned vegetables and fruit, and frozen fruit. Other handy, no-cook staples include canned meats and fish, deli-cooked meats and cold cuts. Use these meats for Ham in Aspic, City Salad or Salade Niçoise.

• For dessert, always have a supply of ice cream (in several flavors), which can be quickly transformed into culinary delights such as parfaits, bombes and sundaes. Dress up your ice cream concoctions with crushed candies, chocolate chips, nuts, candied fruit and whipped cream. With a few extra minutes and ingredients, you can easily turn a little ice cream into Coffee-Toffee Dessert or Spumoni.

So, why not serve Taramasalata, Cold Beef à la Parisienne, Marinated Vegetable Salad and Strawberries Romanoff for an extra special cool dinner? These no-cook recipes are treats for the cook and diners alike.

GINGERED HONEYDEW

1 medium honeydew melon
½ cup sherry

½ cup finely chopped crystallized ginger
mint leaves

1. Halve melon, remove seeds and pare away skin. Slice each half into 4 or 5 long pieces. Cut each piece into several chunks directly into large bowl.

2. Add sherry; toss well. Chill for 2 or 3 hours, tossing occasionally.

3. To serve, arrange melon chunks on 4 small serving plates. Sprinkle each with 2 tablespoons chopped crystallized ginger. Garnish with mint leaves. *Serves 4.*

ENDIVE AND CAVIAR APPETIZER

3 heads Belgian endive
one 8-ounce package cream cheese

1 cup chopped onion
one 3½-ounce jar lumpfish caviar

1. Separate endive heads into leaves. Rinse leaves and dry with paper towels. Arrange leaves wreath fashion around edge of serving plate or tray.

2. Mound cream cheese in center of plate; ring with onion. Spoon caviar on top of cream cheese. *Serves 4.*

AVOCADO WITH SOUR CREAM AND RED CAVIAR

1 small head Boston lettuce
2 avocados
lemon juice

1 cup sour cream
one 5-ounce jar red caviar

1. Core and rinse lettuce; shake dry. Arrange lettuce leaves on 4 salad plates.

2. Cut avocados in half; remove pit but do not peel. Sprinkle with lemon juice to prevent discoloration.

3. Arrange avocado halves on lettuce. Fill each cavity with ¼ cup sour cream. Top with a large spoonful of red caviar. *Serves 4.*

TARAMASALATA

3 slices white bread, crusts removed	**1 egg yolk**
¼ cup water	**1 cup olive oil**
one 5-ounce jar tarama (red roe of cod)	**3 tablespoons lemon juice**
1 tablespoon chopped onion	**warm pita (pocket) bread**

1. Tear white bread into small pieces; soak in ¼ cup water. Place tarama and onion in blender container; process for a few seconds, until pureed.

2. Squeeze bread as dry as possible; add to blender container along with egg yolk. With blender at medium speed, add oil in a steady stream. Add lemon juice. Continue to blend until mixture is smooth.

3. Turn mixture into a bowl and chill until serving time. Serve with wedges of warm pita bread. *Serves 4.*

STEAK TARTARE

2 pounds ground beef sirloin or tenderloin	**8 anchovy fillets, chopped**
2 raw egg yolks	**2 teaspoons Worcestershire sauce**
½ cup finely chopped onion	**salt and pepper to taste**
¼ cup chopped fresh parsley	**lettuce leaves**
1 tablespoon Dijon-style mustard	**pumpernickel bread or hot buttered toast**
1 tablespoon capers, chopped	

1. In large bowl, mix ground beef with egg yolks, onion, parsley, mustard, capers, anchovy fillets, Worcestershire sauce and salt and pepper. Chill for several hours.

2. Shape chilled beef mixture into large flat cake; place on chilled plate. Garnish with lettuce leaves. Serve at once with thin slices of dark pumpernickel or hot buttered toast. *Serves 4.*

Note: Make sure your raw ground meat comes from a very reliable source. The meat grinder should never be used to grind pork or ham.

BIRD'S NEST

6 anchovy fillets, chopped
1 tablespoon chopped parsley
1 tablespoon chopped onion
1 tablespoon capers

1 tablespoon chopped pickled beets
1 raw egg yolk
flat crisp rye bread

1. Place the anchovies, parsley, onion, capers and beets in touching mounds to make a circle, or in concentric circles, on a round serving dish. Gently drop the egg yolk in the center to fill the "nest."

2. To serve, stir the circled ingredients together into the egg yolk until well blended. Spoon mixture onto small squares of flat crisp rye bread. *Serves 4.*

Note: Amounts of ingredients listed are approximate. Use more or less for greater eye appeal.

SUPER SHRIMP DIP

one 10¾-ounce can condensed cream of
   shrimp soup
one 8-ounce package cream cheese,
   softened
½ cup sour cream
1 tablespoon horseradish

1 tablespoon finely chopped onion
½ teaspoon Worcestershire sauce
2 drops hot pepper sauce
two 4½-ounce cans tiny shrimp, drained,
   rinsed and chilled
potato chips or crackers

1. Using electric mixer at medium speed, blend together condensed cream of shrimp soup, cream cheese, sour cream, horseradish, onion, Worcestershire sauce and hot pepper sauce in small bowl.

2. Fold shrimp into soup mixture; chill until ready to serve. Serve with chips or crackers. *Serves 4 to 6.*

CHILLED CURRY SOUP

two 13¾-ounce cans chicken broth
1 tablespoon curry powder
1 tablespoon lemon juice

1 egg yolk
1 cup heavy cream

1. Pour chicken broth into medium bowl; chill for several hours. Skim off fat that rises to the surface.

2. Mix curry powder and lemon juice; stir into broth with wire whisk. Using whisk, beat together egg yolk and heavy cream; beat into broth mixture.

3. Chill soup for several hours. Whip briskly with whisk just before serving. *Serves 4 to 6.*

COLD SPINACH SOUP

one 10-ounce package frozen spinach, thawed
two 10¾-ounce cans chicken broth
½ cup heavy cream

1 egg
2 tablespoons chopped onion
salt and pepper to taste

1. Place thawed spinach in coarse strainer or sieve. Using wooden spoon, press out all of the moisture.

2. Combine spinach, chicken broth, heavy cream, egg and onion in blender container; add salt and pepper.

3. Blend until smooth. Chill until ready to serve; serve in chilled cups. *Serves 4.*

CREAM OF AVOCADO SOUP

2 ripe avocados
1 cup watercress leaves, packed
1½ cups chicken broth
1 cup heavy cream
½ teaspoon salt

⅛ teaspoon onion salt
⅛ teaspoon celery salt
2 teaspoons lemon juice
mint sprigs (optional)

1. Peel, pit and cut up avocados. In electric blender, puree avocados, watercress and chicken broth in two batches. Pour into medium bowl.

2. Blend in heavy cream, salt, onion salt, celery salt and lemon juice. Cover and chill until ready to serve. Garnish with sprigs of mint if available. *Serves 4.*

CUCUMBER SOUP

2 cucumbers, pared and seeded
1 to 1½ cups buttermilk
1 teaspoon salt
⅛ teaspoon pepper

2 tablespoons chopped onion
⅛ teaspoon nutmeg
¼ cup snipped chives

1. Cut cucumbers into chunks. Pour 1 cup of the buttermilk into blender container and add half of the cucumber chunks; process until smooth.

2. Add remaining chunks of cucumber, the salt, pepper, onion and nutmeg. Blend for a few seconds. For thinner soup, add additional ½ cup buttermilk. Chill. Serve in cold cups with a sprinkling of snipped chives. *Serves 4.*

GAZPACHO

3 large tomatoes
1 cucumber
1 green pepper
1 onion
1 clove garlic
two 10½-ounce cans beef consommé
1½ cups tomato juice

⅓ cup wine vinegar
¼ cup olive oil
salt and pepper to taste
small croutons sautéed in oil
chopped tomato, cucumber, green pepper
    and onion

1. Peel and seed the 3 tomatoes and the cucumber; seed the green pepper. Peel the onion and garlic. Cut up vegetables to fit into blender container.

2. In electric blender, combine some of the cut-up vegetables with some consommé. Process in two or three batches at high speed for a few seconds, until pureed.

3. In large bowl, stir together pureed vegetables, remaining consommé, tomato juice, vinegar and olive oil; mix well. Add salt and pepper. Cover and chill. Chill soup cups or bowls at same time.

4. To serve, stir soup well, then spoon into chilled soup cups. Pass separate small bowls of sautéed croutons and chopped tomato, cucumber, green pepper and onion, to be added to taste. *Serves 4.*

COLD SHRIMP SOUP

one 7½-ounce can tiny shrimp
½ cucumber, pared and seeded
1 quart buttermilk
1 tablespoon snipped chives

1 tablespoon Dijon-style mustard
1 teaspoon salt
1 teaspoon sugar

1. Rinse shrimp in cold water, drain and set aside. Finely chop cucumber or puree in electric blender.

2. Combine shrimp, cucumber, buttermilk, chives, mustard, salt and sugar. Mix well and chill until ready to serve. Serve in chilled cups. *Serves 4.*

Note: If buttermilk is not available, add 2 tablespoons white vinegar to ⅞ cup milk. Let stand for 5 to 6 minutes. Stir well before using.

TOMATOES WITH A HEART

4 tomatoes	**⅓ cup sour cream**
salt	**1 teaspoon lemon juice**
4 artichoke hearts, drained	**1 teaspoon curry powder**
(from a 4-ounce can)	**fresh spinach leaves**
1 cup mayonnaise	**chopped parsley or chives**

1. Cut a slice from the top of each tomato. Use a spoon to scoop out some tomato pulp, leaving a cavity just big enough for an artichoke heart. Salt tomato well and invert to drain for 30 minutes.

2. Place an artichoke heart in each drained tomato; chill until ready to serve.

3. In a small bowl, mix mayonnaise, sour cream, lemon juice and curry powder. Chill until ready to use.

4. At serving time, arrange tomatoes on a bed of crisp fresh spinach leaves. Top each tomato with a swirl of curry dressing. Sprinkle with chopped parsley or chives. *Serves 4.*

CUCUMBER SALAD

4 cucumbers	**1 teaspoon sugar**
salt	**2 tablespoons snipped chives**
½ cup vinegar	**2 tablespoons chopped onion**
½ cup oil	

1. Pare cucumbers and slice paper thin into a medium bowl. Salt heavily and place a heavy plate on top, pressing on the cucumber slices. Chill several hours.

2. Combine vinegar, oil and sugar in a screwtop jar; shake vigorously and chill.

3. Turn the cucumber slices into a strainer; press hard to extract as much liquid as possible.

4. Return slices to bowl, mix in chives and onion. Shake dressing vigorously; pour over cucumbers and toss gently. Chill until ready to serve. *Serves 4.*

EnergySaving Tip: Tomatoes are at their best in late summer and early fall; serving vine-ripened tomatoes in season does away with the need to cook them. When serving raw cucumbers, look for the English-style garden cucumbers with their thin, ridged skins; they have an interesting, delicate flavor and do not need peeling. It is always worthwhile to thinly slice, salt and drain cucumbers; they become crisper and absorb dressing without diluting it with cucumber liquid. Once they're tossed with dressing, cucumbers should be served immediately as they do not remain crisp for long. Cucumbers are available throughout the year, but they are most flavorful in summer.

ENDIVE SALAD

6 heads Belgian endive (about 1 pound)
⅓ cup vinegar
2 tablespoons olive or vegetable oil

1 teaspoon Dijon-style mustard
salt and pepper to taste
¾ cup chopped parsley

1. Rinse, then cut endive into long, fine julienne strips. Wrap in paper towels; place in plastic bag and chill.

2. Pour vinegar and oil into screwtop jar; add mustard, salt and pepper. Shake vigorously and chill.

3. To serve, combine endive and parsley in glass bowl. Toss with dressing and serve at once. *Serves 4.*

BEAN SPROUT AND SPINACH SALAD

one 16-ounce can bean sprouts, drained
    and rinsed
½ pound fresh spinach, rinsed, dried and
    stems removed
½ cup thinly sliced water chestnuts
½ cup peanut oil

¼ cup soy sauce
2 tablespoons lemon juice
1 teaspoon sugar
¼ teaspoon pepper
⅛ teaspoon onion salt
2 tablespoons toasted sesame seeds

1. Cover bean sprouts with cold water and chill for several hours to crisp sprouts and freshen flavor. Rinse and drain again before using.

2. Wrap spinach in paper towels; put in plastic bag, along with water chestnuts, and chill until ready to serve.

3. Mix peanut oil, soy sauce, lemon juice, sugar, pepper and onion salt in screwtop jar; shake vigorously.

4. In salad bowl, combine bean sprouts, spinach and water chestnuts. Add dressing and toss gently but thoroughly. Sprinkle with toasted sesame seeds and serve at once. *Serves 4.*

COLESLAW

1 firm head cabbage
¾ cup mayonnaise
¼ cup sour cream

2 tablespoons lemon juice
1 tablespoon caraway seeds
salt and freshly ground pepper to taste

1. Halve the cabbage and remove hard core. Grate, shred or finely chop cabbage to measure 6 cups; place in large bowl. Cover with ice cubes and water; chill several hours.

2. In small bowl, mix mayonnaise, sour cream, lemon juice, caraway seeds, salt and pepper.

3. Thoroughly drain cabbage; toss with mayonnaise dressing and chill. *Serves 6.*

MOTHER-IN-LAW SALAD

1 cup boiling water
one 3-ounce package lemon-flavored
    gelatin
1 cup cold water
1 tablespoon onion juice
1 tablespoon vinegar

salt and pepper to taste
½ cup grated carrot
½ cup chopped celery
lettuce leaves
mayonnaise

1. In large bowl, stir 1 cup boiling water into lemon gelatin until gelatin dissolves. Stir in 1 cup cold water, the onion juice and vinegar. Chill until thickened, 30 to 45 minutes, stirring occasionally.

2. Add salt and pepper to thickened gelatin mixture. Fold in carrot and celery.

3. Rinse four 10-ounce custard cups with cold water. Spoon salad into cups. Chill until firm, about 1 hour.

4. Loosen salad in cups by running sharp knife around edges of mold. Invert onto 4 lettuce-lined salad plates. Shake to release. Serve with mayonnaise. *Serves 4.*

MARINATED VEGETABLE SALAD

½ small head cauliflower, cut into
    flowerets
½ small head broccoli, cut into flowerets
one 4-ounce jar marinated artichoke
    hearts, drained
one 3-ounce jar pitted black olives,
    drained
1 cup thickly sliced celery (½-inch slices)
1 cup julienne strips carrot
1 cup julienne strips green pepper
½ cup halved cherry tomatoes

DRESSING
¾ cup wine vinegar
½ cup olive oil
1 tablespoon chopped parsley
1 teaspoon salt
½ teaspoon dry mustard
¼ teaspoon oregano
¼ teaspoon tarragon or chervil

1. In large bowl, mix together all vegetables. Add a handful of ice cubes and refrigerate.

2. Make dressing: Combine vinegar, oil, parsley, salt, dry mustard, oregano, and tarragon or chervil in screwtop jar. Shake vigorously to blend.

3. Drain vegetables, removing ice cubes. Add enough dressing to coat vegetables thoroughly. Refrigerate overnight. Serve very cold with extra dressing alongside. *Serves 4 to 6.*

KIDNEY BEAN SALAD

one 16-ounce can red kidney beans
½ cup vinegar
3 tablespoons oil
¼ teaspoon dry mustard

½ teaspoon salt
¼ teaspoon pepper
½ cup onion rings
chopped parsley

1. Rinse beans under cold running water; drain well. Place in medium bowl. Add vinegar and oil; chill for 2 to 3 hours, stirring several times.

2. Stir in dry mustard, salt and pepper; mix well. To serve, garnish with onion rings and parsley. *Serves 4.*

COLD BEEF A LA PARISIENNE

French Dressing (below)
1 pound thinly sliced cooked roast beef
1 large onion
1 small head iceberg or romaine lettuce

1 pint store-bought German potato salad
1 tomato, cut into small wedges
chopped parsley

1. Make French Dressing. Sprinkle each slice of roast beef with a little of the dressing and roll up from the short side jelly-roll fashion. Arrange rolls side by side in shallow dish.

2. Slice onion and separate into rings. Spread onion rings over beef rolls. Spoon 3 to 4 tablespoons dressing over all. Cover and let stand for 30 minutes or until ready to serve.

3. At serving time, break up or shred lettuce; spread on serving platter. Arrange rolls down center of platter, topped with onion rings. Surround with spoonfuls of potato salad, alternating with tomato wedges. Sprinkle with parsley. Spoon a little dressing over all; serve remaining dressing alongside. *Serves 4.*

French Dressing

2 tablespoons vinegar
6 tablespoons vegetable or olive oil
pinch of salt

¼ teaspoon dry mustard
freshly ground pepper to taste

1. In screwtop jar, combine vinegar, oil, salt, dry mustard and pepper.

2. Shake vigorously to blend. Use at once to dress salad. *Makes ½ cup.*

Note: This dressing stores indefinitely; shake before using.

CITY SALAD

one 12-ounce can corned beef
one 16-ounce can whole potatoes,
   drained
1 cup chopped celery
½ cup mayonnaise
1 tablespoon vinegar

salt and pepper to taste
lettuce leaves
2 tomatoes, cut into wedges
½ cup stuffed olives
½ cup chopped parsley

1. Using sharp knife, cut corned beef into small cubes. Dice the drained potatoes. In large bowl, combine corned beef, potatoes and celery.

2. Add mayonnaise, vinegar, salt and pepper. Toss gently, until well blended.

3. Serve on bed of lettuce leaves, surrounded by wreath of tomato wedges, olives and parsley. *Serves 4.*

HAM IN ASPIC

1 envelope unflavored gelatin
¾ cup water
one 10½-ounce can beef consommé
2 cups finely chopped precooked ham
½ cup chopped celery

1 tablespoon lemon juice
salt and pepper to taste
lettuce leaves
mayonnaise

1. In large bowl, soften gelatin in ¼ cup of the water. Boil remaining ½ cup water; pour over softened gelatin. Stir to dissolve; stir in beef consommé. Chill gelatin mixture until thickened, about 30 minutes.

2. Fold ham, celery, lemon juice, salt and pepper into thickened mixture; mix well. Rinse 8½ x 4½ x 2½-inch loaf pan with cold water; spoon in gelatin mixture. Chill for several hours or until firm.

3. Line oblong serving dish or tray with lettuce leaves. Loosen edges of mold with sharp knife. Dip mold quickly into hot water, then invert on lettuce leaves; shake to release. Serve aspic with mayonnaise. *Serves 4.*

CURRIED CHICKEN SALAD

**3 cups cubed cooked chicken, or 1½
   pounds precooked chicken roll, cubed,
   or three 6¾-ounce cans chicken chunks**
1 cup diced celery
2 tablespoons raisins
2 tablespoons oil and vinegar dressing
½ cup mayonnaise

1 tablespoon lemon juice
½ teaspoon curry powder
salt and pepper to taste
lettuce cups
**one 4-ounce can mandarin oranges,
   drained**

1. In medium bowl, toss to combine chicken, celery, raisins and oil and vinegar dressing; cover with plastic wrap. Let stand for 1 hour.

2. In small bowl, blend mayonnaise, lemon juice, curry powder, salt and pepper. Add mayonnaise mixture to chicken mixture; mix gently but thoroughly.

3. To serve, heap chicken salad into lettuce cups. Garnish with drained mandarin oranges. *Serves 4 to 6.*

TURKEY WALDORF SALAD

1 unpeeled red apple, diced
1 tablespoon lemon juice
**3 cups diced cooked turkey, or 1½
   pounds precooked turkey roll, diced**
1 cup red grapes, halved and seeded

1 cup diced celery
⅓ cup coarsely chopped walnuts
¾ cup mayonnaise
salt and pepper to taste
lettuce leaves

1. Sprinkle diced apple with lemon juice to prevent discoloration.

2. In medium bowl, mix apple, turkey, grapes, celery and walnuts. Toss with mayonnaise; add salt and pepper. Serve on lettuce leaves. *Serves 4.*

SALADE NICOISE

1 head Boston lettuce, rinsed and dried
**one 7-ounce can chunk-style tuna,
   drained**
2 tomatoes, quartered
½ cup pitted black olives

one 2-ounce can anchovy fillets, drained
2 hard-cooked eggs, sliced
½ pint store-bought German potato salad
1 tablespoon chopped parsley
½ cup bottled garlic dressing

1. Arrange lettuce leaves around edge of shallow salad bowl or serving platter. Tear or chop unused leaves and spread in center of bowl.

2. Arrange tuna chunks, tomato wedges, olives, anchovies and sliced eggs on lettuce in circles, triangles or other attractive pattern around edge of bowl. Place potato salad in center.

3. Sprinkle with chopped parsley and present at table, with dressing alongside. When ready to serve, toss lightly but well with dressing. *Serves 4.*

AVOCADO CRAB LOUIS

1 cup Louis Dressing (below)
2 or 3 heads Bibb lettuce
2 avocados, halved and pitted
lemon juice
2 cups cooked crabmeat (fresh or frozen)

2 tomatoes, cut into thin wedges
1 cup pitted black olives
¼ cup snipped chives
2 hard-cooked eggs, cut into wedges

1. Prepare Louis Dressing; chill.

2. Line a platter with lettuce. Arrange avocado halves on lettuce; sprinkle with lemon juice to prevent discoloration.

3. Pick over crabmeat, discarding any membranes or cartilage. Toss crabmeat with chilled dressing; heap into avocado halves.

4. Garnish platter with tomato wedges, whole or sliced olives, snipped chives and wedges of egg. *Serves 4. (Shown on page 49.)*

Louis Dressing

¼ cup heavy cream
1 cup mayonnaise
¼ cup chili sauce
2 tablespoons chopped green pepper

2 tablespoons chopped green onion
1½ teaspoons Worcestershire sauce
1 teaspoon lemon juice
½ teaspoon salt

1. Beat heavy cream until stiff. In medium bowl, stir together mayonnaise, chili sauce, green pepper, green onion, Worcestershire sauce, lemon juice and salt.

2. Thoroughly mix ingredients, then fold into stiffly beaten heavy cream. Chill about 30 minutes before combining with crabmeat. *Makes about 2 cups.*

EnergySaving Tip: It's often small ideas that can save a great deal of energy. If you are preparing hard-cooked eggs ahead of time, boil them for only 5 minutes (covered, of course, to minimize the heat in your kitchen). Remove from the heat and let stand in the pot of hot water for about 25 minutes before cracking the shells under cold running water. Follow these other energy-saving tips when making salads:
• Buy precooked meats from the supermarket or delicatessen. Sliced turkey or chicken roll is an excellent buy, as is chunk-style turkey or chicken. Corned beef and pastrami are well worth the money for a change of menu and savings in cooking energy.
• Store-bought vegetable salads are another way to save energy. Potatoes, especially, take time to cook at home and are usually excellent in a delicatessen salad.
• When chopping vegetables in the food processor or blender, chop extra for the freezer; freeze them tightly wrapped in plastic wrap inside an airtight container. The best vegetables to store this way are onions (green onions, too), and green and red peppers; the best herbs to store frozen are chopped parsley, chives and basil.

MEDITERRANEAN SALAD

¾ cup olive or vegetable oil
¼ cup fresh lemon juice
¼ teaspoon dry mustard
1 tablespoon snipped chives
1 clove garlic, crushed
salt and pepper to taste
1 pound fresh or frozen (and thawed)
  lump crabmeat
8 large boiled shrimp, shelled, deveined
  and chilled

2 heads Boston lettuce
4 oysters or clams on half shell
2 tablespoons red or black caviar
one 7¾-ounce can salmon, drained and
  flaked (bones removed)
1 ripe avocado, peeled, pitted and
  quartered
2 tablespoons capers
1 large ripe tomato, cut into wedges
8 radishes

1. Combine oil, lemon juice, dry mustard, chives, garlic, salt and pepper in screwtop jar. Shake vigorously to blend; chill.

2. Pick over crabmeat, removing membrane and cartilage. Place in small bowl, moisten with a little dressing. Heap shrimp on top; brush with a little dressing. Cover and chill.

3. Coarsely shred lettuce; sprinkle with some dressing. Divide lettuce among 4 dinner plates.

4. On each bed of lettuce, arrange a mound of crabmeat, 2 shrimp, 1 oyster or clam on half shell topped with generous swirl of caviar, a mound of salmon and a wedge of avocado topped with capers.

5. Garnish with tomato wedges and radishes. Sprinkle all with dressing just before serving. Pass remaining dressing separately. *Serves 4. (Shown on front cover.)*

SHRIMP SALAD MOLD

2 envelopes unflavored gelatin
¼ cup cold water
1 cup boiling water
2 beef bouillon cubes
three 4½-ounce cans tiny shrimp, drained
¼ cup mayonnaise

¼ cup heavy cream, stiffly beaten
2 tablespoons lemon juice
1 tablespoon chopped parsley
1 teaspoon horseradish
lettuce
parsley sprigs

1. In medium bowl, soften gelatin in ¼ cup cold water; stir in 1 cup boiling water and the bouillon cubes. Stir until bouillon cubes are completely dissolved. Chill until mixture is consistency of unbeaten egg whites, 30 to 45 minutes.

2. Fold drained shrimp, mayonnaise, stiffly beaten heavy cream, lemon juice, chopped parsley and horseradish into thickened gelatin mixture. Turn into oiled 4- or 5-cup mold; chill for several hours or overnight.

3. To serve, loosen edges of mold with sharp knife; dip quickly in hot water, shake to release and unmold on a bed of lettuce. Garnish with parsley sprigs. *Serves 4.*

CRAB MOUSSE

1 envelope unflavored gelatin	**2 tablespoons chopped onion**
2 tablespoons lemon juice	**2 tablespoons chopped parsley**
½ cup boiling water	**1 cup canned or frozen (and thawed)**
1 egg	**crabmeat**
⅓ cup mayonnaise	**1 cup light cream**
½ cup chopped celery	**lettuce leaves**

1. In electric blender, combine gelatin, lemon juice and ½ cup boiling water. Process at high speed for 30 seconds. Add egg and blend for 20 seconds.

2. Add mayonnaise, and chopped celery, onion and parsley. Cover and blend at high speed for a few seconds.

3. Drain and pick over crabmeat, removing cartilage and membranes. Add to blender container along with light cream. Blend at high speed for a few seconds until smooth.

4. Turn crab mixture into an oiled 1-quart mold. Chill for several hours or overnight.

5. Unmold on lettuce-lined plate. *Serves 4.*

Note: For Tuna Mousse, use one 7-ounce can tuna in water, drained, instead of crabmeat.

SALMON MOUSSE

1 envelope unflavored gelatin	**½ teaspoon dried dill**
2 tablespoons lemon juice	**1 cup sour cream**
2 tablespoons chopped onion	**lettuce**
½ cup boiling water	**Green Mayonnaise (below)**
½ cup mayonnaise	
one 16-ounce can salmon, drained, flaked	
and bones removed	

1. Combine gelatin, lemon juice, onion and ½ cup boiling water in blender container; process at high speed for 30 seconds.

2. Add mayonnaise, salmon and dill. Process at high speed for a few seconds until smooth. Add sour cream and blend a few seconds.

3. Pour salmon mixture into an oiled 1-quart mold; chill several hours or until firm.

4. Unmold on lettuce and serve with Green Mayonnaise. *Serves 4 to 6.*

Green Mayonnaise

2 teaspoons chopped fresh parsley	**½ teaspoon chopped fresh tarragon**
½ teaspoon chopped fresh chervil	**1½ cups mayonnaise**

1. Stir parsley, chervil and tarragon into mayonnaise.

2. Cover and chill for an hour or more to blend flavors. *Makes 1½ cups.*

CHERRY-MINCEMEAT SALAD

one 16-ounce can pitted dark sweet
   cherries
1½ cups boiling water
three 3-ounce packages cherry-flavored
   gelatin
1 tablespoon lemon juice

½ cup prepared mincemeat
½ cup chopped nuts
¼ cup diced unpeeled apple
¼ cup diced orange (including rind)
lettuce leaves

1. Drain cherry juice into 2-cup measure and add enough water to make 2 cups liquid; set aside. Chop cherries and set aside.

2. Pour 1½ cups boiling water over cherry gelatin in large bowl. Stir until gelatin is dissolved. Stir in lemon juice and reserved cherry juice mixture. Chill mixture until thickened, 30 to 45 minutes.

3. Fold reserved chopped cherries, mincemeat, nuts, apple and orange into thickened mixture. Pour into oiled 5-cup mold; chill until firm, about 2 to 3 hours. To serve, turn out onto lettuce-lined plate. *Serves 8.*

FRESH FRUIT SALAD WITH FRUIT DRESSING

1 large pineapple (or 2 small ones)
½ cup fresh or frozen (and thawed)
   blueberries
½ cup watermelon balls
½ cup halved strawberries

½ cup seedless green grapes
1 banana, peeled and sliced
1 peach, peeled and sliced
Sweet Fruit Salad Dressing (page 25)
mint sprigs (optional)

1. Cut large pineapple in half straight through leaves and fruit, then cut halves in half again to make 4 quarters. (If using small pineapples, cut each in half through leaves and fruit.) Cut pineapple away from shells and cube into large bowl; reserve shells.

2. Add blueberries, watermelon balls, strawberries, grapes, banana and peach to pineapple cubes; toss gently to mix. Chill.

3. To serve, pile chilled fruit into reserved shells. Serve with Sweet Fruit Salad Dressing, and garnish with mint sprigs if desired. *Serves 4.*

Sweet Fruit Salad Dressing

1 cup sliced strawberries
3 tablespoons honey

¾ cup mayonnaise

1. In small bowl, mash sliced strawberries with honey. Stir in mayonnaise; chill for about 30 minutes.

2. Pass dressing with fruit salad. *Makes about 2 cups.*

ICY LIME CANTALOUPES

2 small ripe cantaloupes
1 pint lime sherbet

¼ cup orange-flavored liqueur or
orange juice

1. Cut cantaloupes in half and remove seeds; chill.

2. When ready to serve, place a scoop of lime sherbet in each half; pour 1 tablespoon orange-flavored liqueur or orange juice over each scoop of sherbet and top with a little sprig of mint. *Serves 4.*

STRAWBERRIES ROMANOFF

½ cup unflavored yogurt
2 tablespoons honey
2 tablespoons orange-flavored liqueur or
sherry

1 teaspoon vanilla extract
½ cup heavy cream
1 pint fresh strawberries, hulled

1. In a medium bowl, mix yogurt, honey, liqueur or sherry, and vanilla extract.

2. Whip heavy cream until stiff, then fold into yogurt mixture. Chill until ready to serve, up to 3 or 4 hours.

3. To serve, spoon a generous swirl into each of 4 dessert bowls; top with fresh berries. *Serves 4.*

STRAWBERRY SOUFFLE FROID

2 pints strawberries
2 envelopes unflavored gelatin
1 cup sugar
½ cup boiling water

2 tablespoons lemon juice
1 tablespoon kirsch
3 egg whites
1 cup heavy cream

1. Rinse and hull strawberries; reserve a few for garnish. Puree remaining strawberries in electric blender.

2. In medium bowl, mix gelatin into ½ cup of the sugar. Add ½ cup boiling water; stir until gelatin dissolves. Add strawberry puree, lemon juice and kirsch. Chill, stirring mixture occasionally, until it begins to thicken and mound slightly, about 30 minutes.

3. Using electric mixer at high speed, beat egg whites until soft peaks form; add remaining ½ cup sugar, 1 tablespoon at a time, beating continuously until stiff peaks form.

4. Using electric mixer at high speed, beat heavy cream until stiff. Fold whipped cream into strawberry mixture, then fold in egg whites. Pour into 2-quart soufflé or serving dish. Chill for 3 to 4 hours. Garnish with reserved berries. *Serves 4 to 6.*

COEUR A LA CREME

three 8-ounce containers small curd
   cottage cheese
2 cups light cream

1¼ cups sugar
¼ teaspoon salt
1 quart fresh strawberries

1. In a medium bowl, beat the cottage cheese with an electric or hand mixer until smooth. Gradually add the light cream, beating continuously.

2. Stir in ¼ cup of the sugar and the salt. Turn the mixture into a sieve or strainer lined with cheesecloth; place over a bowl and refrigerate for at least 24 hours to drain.

3. Rinse, hull and slice strawberries. Reserve a few whole berries for garnish. Mix sliced berries with the remaining 1 cup of sugar. Chill.

4. When ready to serve, turn cheese out on serving dish (it will hold its shape). Garnish with reserved whole berries. Heap the sliced berries around the molded cheese, or pass separately in a bowl. *Serves 4. (Shown on page 88.)*

Note: There is a heart-shaped china mold with holes in the bottom made for this dessert. Line 1½-quart mold with cheesecloth; press cheese mixture into mold. Set mold on plate. Place in refrigerator to drain. Serve as directed.

BANANA SHERBET

2 ripe bananas	**1 cup sugar**
⅓ cup orange juice	**2 eggs**
¼ cup lemon juice	**1½ cups water**

1. Cut bananas in chunks. In electric blender, puree bananas with orange juice, lemon juice and sugar until smooth.

2. Add eggs and 1½ cups water. Process until very smooth. Pour into ice cube trays; freeze until almost solid, about 1 hour.

3. Turn banana mixture into large bowl of electric mixer, break up into small pieces and beat until smooth and slushy.

4. Spoon mixture into a 1-quart plastic container, cover and freeze until firm, about 1½ to 2 hours. *Serves 4.*

SPUMONI

1 quart strawberry ice cream, softened	**¼ cup diced mixed candied fruit**
1 pint pistachio ice cream, softened	**2 tablespoons rum**
1 pint vanilla ice cream, softened	**1 cup heavy cream, stiffly beaten**

1. Place a 1½-quart melon mold in the freezer for at least 3 hours before starting this dessert. Use any flavors of ice cream you prefer, but this combination is particularly good.

2. Stir or beat the strawberry ice cream until thick and smooth, but *not* melted. Work quickly and line the frozen mold with about a 1-inch-thick layer of ice cream; freeze until firm, about 1 hour.

3. Repeat with pistachio ice cream, spreading a 1-inch layer over the first layer; freeze until firm, about 30 minutes.

4. Stir or beat vanilla ice cream; blend in candied fruit and rum. Fill center of mold with this mixture; freeze until firm, about 30 minutes.

5. To unmold, dip mold in warm water for a minute or two, invert on platter and shake loose. Return platter to freezer for 5 to 10 minutes. Decorate with stiffly beaten heavy cream, piped through a pastry tube. *Serves 8.*

FROZEN DEMITASSE DESSERTS

1 cup cold strong coffee
½ cup Irish whiskey
2 cups heavy cream

2 cups light cream
nutmeg

1. In a large bowl, mix coffee, whiskey, heavy and light cream. Blend with a hand beater until just slightly thickened.

2. Pour into ice cube trays and freeze until firm, about 1½ to 2 hours.

3. Spoon frozen mixture into demitasse cups. Serve with a sprinkling of nutmeg. *Serves 8.*

COFFEE-TOFFEE DESSERT

2 quarts coffee ice cream
2 cups crushed chocolate wafers

2 cups crushed chocolate-toffee
candy bars

1. Remove ice cream from freezer and allow to soften while preparing remainder of dessert.

2. Reserve ⅓ cup of the chocolate wafer crumbs for garnish; sprinkle remainder on the bottom of a 13 x 9 x 2-inch baking dish.

3. Fold the crushed chocolate-toffee candy into the softened ice cream. Spread ice cream over crumbs in dish. Smooth over top surface of ice cream and sprinkle with reserved crumbs.

4. Freeze ice cream several hours or overnight. Cut into 3-inch squares. *Serves 12.*

BISCUIT TORTONI

3 eggs, separated
¾ cup confectioners' sugar
2 tablespoons sherry

1 teaspoon vanilla extract
1½ cups heavy cream, stiffly beaten
½ cup crushed macaroons

1. In a medium bowl, beat egg yolks and confectioners' sugar until thick and light. Beat in sherry and vanilla extract. Thoroughly wash and dry beaters.

2. In another medium bowl, beat egg whites until they are stiff but not dry.

3. Gently fold stiffly beaten heavy cream into egg whites, sprinkling and folding in most of the macaroon crumbs at the same time. Set aside a generous tablespoon of the crumbs for garnish.

4. Gently fold in egg yolk mixture. Spoon mixture into paper cups or short-stemmed dessert dishes. Sprinkle with reserved crumbs and freeze for several hours. *Serves 4 to 6.*

ICEBOX COOKIE DESSERT

1 cup heavy cream
1 cup apple butter or apple jelly

20 vanilla wafers, chocolate wafers or
gingersnaps

1. Using electric mixer at high speed, beat heavy cream in large bowl until soft peaks form. Beat apple butter or jelly into cream, 1 tablespoon at a time, until stiff. Do not overbeat.

2. Stack 10 cookies, spreading apple-cream mixture between each cookie. Repeat with remaining cookies and filling to make 2 stacks in all. (Reserve some of the apple-cream mixture for frosting.)

3. On narrow, oblong serving platter, gently tip cookie stacks to lie side by side. Frost completely with remaining apple-cream mixture. Chill for 2 hours.

4. To serve, cut slightly on the diagonal into ½-inch slices. *Serves 4.*

CHEESECAKE JAMAICA

¼ cup cold water or coffee
2 envelopes unflavored gelatin
½ cup boiling water
¾ cup brown sugar, firmly packed
¼ teaspoon salt
three 8-ounce containers creamed
** cottage cheese**

2 eggs, separated
1½ tablespoons instant coffee
1 tablespoon rum
one 14½-ounce can evaporated milk,
** chilled**
½ to ¾ cup graham cracker crumbs

1. Put cold water or coffee and gelatin into blender container. Allow to soften for a few minutes. Add ½ cup boiling water, the brown sugar and salt. Process until gelatin is dissolved and mixture is smooth.

2. Add cottage cheese, egg yolks, instant coffee and rum. Blend until smooth.

3. In a small bowl, beat egg whites until they form soft peaks. Using electric mixer, beat evaporated milk in small bowl until it forms soft peaks.

4. Pour blender mixture into a large mixing bowl. Add beaten evaporated milk and fold in. Add beaten egg whites and fold in.

5. Pour or spoon cheesecake mixture into an 8-inch springform pan. Sprinkle top with graham cracker crumbs. Chill for 2 to 3 hours or until set and firm. *Serves 8.*

SICILIAN CASSATA

one 9-ounce frozen pound cake, thawed
one 16-ounce container ricotta or cottage
  cheese
3 tablespoons sugar
3 tablespoons orange- or almond-flavored
  liqueur
¼ cup coarsely chopped semisweet
  chocolate

2 tablespoons coarsely chopped mixed
  candied fruit
2 tablespoons strong coffee
one 16½-ounce can ready-to-spread
  chocolate frosting, or one 15¼-ounce
  package chocolate frosting mix

1. Cut pound cake horizontally into 5 or 6 even slices. If the top of the cake is very rounded, cut it flat.

2. Using an electric or hand mixer, beat ricotta or cottage cheese in a medium bowl until it is smooth and light. While beating, add sugar and liqueur. Fold in the semisweet chocolate and candied fruit.

3. Place the bottom slice of cake on serving dish; spread with the cheese mixture. Alternate layers of cake and cheese filling, using all of the filling. End with a layer of cake. Chill for several hours, or until firm.

4. Thoroughly stir the coffee into the ready-to-spread chocolate frosting, or use the coffee as part of the liquid called for to prepare the frosting mix. Cover the cake with frosting, swirling it attractively on top and sides.

5. Cover the cake loosely with aluminum foil or plastic wrap. Chill for a day or overnight before slicing. *Serves 6 to 8.*

EnergySaving Tip: Frozen baked goods are the biggest energy-savers of all, since they eliminate the need to switch on a large oven for the better part of an hour. Thawing baked goods at room temperature saves energy, but for those in a hurry, a few minutes in the microwave will also do the trick. Follow these other energy-saving tips when making desserts:
• Always use very ripe fruit or canned fruit for pie fillings; there's no need, then, for lengthy simmering.
• Look for pre-packaged individual sponge cake shells to serve as containers for fruit and cream desserts, rather than baking your own.
• Experiment with unusual flavors to add extra taste to cool and simple desserts. Slow-simmered mincemeat comes in a jar, ready to serve; it's a rich and flavorful addition to any frozen parfait. Creamy, luxurious chestnuts are a similar energy-saving convenience; they are available packed in jars and cans, either whole (in syrup) or pureed.
• Refrigerators and freezers use energy, too. To operate them most efficiently, place only cool (not hot) food in them. Open the doors as little as possible while desserts are chilling or freezing.

MONT BLANC

two 16-ounce cans chestnut puree, chilled	**1 tablespoon vanilla extract**
1 cup heavy cream	**1 tablespoon sugar**
	powdered sugar

1. Put the chestnut puree through a ricer twice. On the second time, let the spaghetti-like strands pile up in a ring on a serving plate.

2. Beat heavy cream with the vanilla extract and 1 tablespoon sugar until stiff. Pile whipped cream in center of chestnut puree ring.

3. Just before serving, sprinkle chestnut puree with a little powdered sugar. *Serves 4 to 6.*

ENGLISH TRIFLE

one 3-ounce package instant vanilla pudding	**1 cup heavy cream**
one 9-ounce frozen pound cake, thawed	**¼ cup sugar**
½ cup raspberry jam	**1 teaspoon vanilla extract**
½ cup sherry	**¼ cup toasted slivered almonds**

1. Prepare instant pudding according to label directions. Slice cake into 3 horizontal layers.

2. Spread 2 of the layers with jam and reassemble the pound cake; cut vertically into jam "sandwiches." Arrange on bottom of serving bowl, cutting to fit if necessary.

3. Sprinkle sherry over cake and let stand 10 minutes. Spread vanilla pudding over cake. Cover with plastic wrap and chill overnight.

4. When ready to serve, beat heavy cream with sugar and vanilla extract until stiff. Spread over pudding layer in bowl; sprinkle with almonds. *Serves 4 to 6.*

EnergySaving Tip: Instant puddings always save energy; an even quicker alternative is to use individual serving sizes of canned vanilla pudding. Consider these substitutions for the English Trifle recipe:
• Use sponge ladyfingers instead of pound cake; split them, fill with jam, and then sandwich them together.
• Apricot or strawberry jams are just as tasty as raspberry jam, and they impart a traditional flavor to the dessert.
• Use a rich cream sherry to give a pronounced nut-sweet tang to the cake layer in the bottom of the bowl. If you can find them, try Madeira or Marsala wine; they're even better. And a tablespoon or two of wine instead of vanilla extract can be beaten into the heavy cream, if you wish.
• Even the type of nut used to garnish the trifle will add varying dimensions of flavor. If you use the deeper dark sherries, consider a sprinkle of walnuts, or even hazelnuts or filberts.
• A few words on cream and some substitutes: Rich and smooth heavy cream is without peer; refrigerator dessert topping is ready to use and lower in calories; even lower in calories is chilled evaporated milk (whipped to frothy stiffness). Whip the evaporated milk at the last moment; it loses its stiffness quickly.

HERBS AND SPICES

	ALLSPICE	BASIL	CHILI	CINNAMON	DILL	GARLIC
	Whole or ground, combines fragrance of cinnamon, cloves and nutmeg. Very pungent; use sparingly, adding as taste indicates.	Excellent fresh, best bought rooted in pots; when dried, the leaves crumble finely. Fresh, savory-sweet flavor; use generously.	Made from dried and finely ground hot chili peppers; often said to be America's version of curry powder. While they are very different flavors, chili and curry can often be used interchangeably.	The bark of a tree; commonly bought powdered, but also comes in the form of a cinnamon stick. To be used in both sweet and savory dishes; strongly aromatic, so use sparingly.	A mildly pungent herb of the parsley family; both seeds and leaves are used to season food. The seeds are only available dried; the leaves (called dill weed) are available both fresh and dried.	A small, pungent, onionlike bulb; a whole bulb consists of many cloves. Best used fresh, it is also available in dehydrated, instant-minced form, or as garlic salt or garlic powder.
SOUPS AND SAUCES	Fish Soups Barbecue Sauces Fruit Sauces Pickles and Relishes	Chicken and Turkey Soups Fish Soups Vegetable Soups Fish and Poultry Sauces	Bean Soups Green Pea Soups Lentil Soups Meat Gravies	Chilled Beef and Tomato Soups Summer Fruit Soups Beef Gravies	Cold Creamed Soups Green Pea Soups Tomato Soups Fish Sauces	Onion Soups Bean Soups Beef Soups Meat Gravies
SALADS AND SALAD DRESSINGS	Fruit Salads Sweet-Sour Dressings	Chicken Salads Seafood Salads Cucumber and Tomato Salads Vinaigrette Dressings	Guacamoles Avocado Salads Fruit Salads Potato Salads	Cottage Cheese Salads Fruit Salads Molded Salads	Green Bean Vinaigrettes Cucumber Salads Potato Salads Mayonnaise Sour Cream Dressings	Beef Vinaigrettes Shellfish Salads Potato Salads Three-Bean Salads
MEAT MAIN DISHES	Beef Stews Ground Beef Dishes Ham and Pork Dishes	Beef Stews Lamb Roasts and Stews Pork Stuffings	Barbecued Meats Chili and Curry Dishes Ham and Pork Dishes	Beef Stews Sauerbraten Roast Ham Pork Chops	Lamb Chops and Roasts Swedish Meatballs Veal Roasts	Beef Pot Roasts Ground Beef Dishes Roast Lamb
EGGS, POULTRY AND SEAFOOD	Scrambled Eggs Creamed Chicken Fish Stews	Omelets Scrambled Eggs Roast Chicken Fish Fillets	Scrambled Eggs Shellfish Dishes Chicken and Turkey Dishes	Chicken Fricassee Creamed Turkey	Creamed Egg Dishes Salmon Shellfish Seafood Stuffings	Roast Chicken Scampi Poultry Stuffings
PASTA AND VEGETABLES	Carrots Parsnips Squash Sweet Potatoes	Pastas Pizzas Green and Wax Beans Tomatoes Zucchini	Corn Lima and Dried Beans Acorn and Butternut Squash Tomatoes	Carrots Onions Acorn and Butternut Squash Sweet Potatoes	Broccoli Cabbage Cauliflower Peas	Tomato Sauces for Pastas Pizzas Bean Casseroles
BAKED GOODS AND DESSERTS	Coffee Cakes Fruit Cakes Poached Fresh Fruits	Cheese Breads Garlic Breads	Savory Biscuits and Breads	Coffee Cakes Nut Breads and Cakes Sweet Rolls	Cheese Breads Onion Breads	Cheese Biscuits Herb Breads
BEVERAGES	Iced Tea Apple Cider			Iced and Hot Coffee Tea Chocolate		

MINT	NUTMEG	OREGANO	PARSLEY	POPPY SEEDS	SAGE	THYME
A pungent, aromatic herb; sold fresh in bunches in late spring through summer. When dried, the leaves crumble finely; use in both sweet and savory dishes.	The seed of a fruit, similar to mace in flavor. Best if bought whole and grated as needed; more commonly found powdered. Use sparingly in both sweet and savory dishes.	An aromatic, pungent herb with tiny leaves; common to the Mediterranean. Found fresh in pots; more frequently dried. Use with some restraint.	The most popular herb, available fresh all year round; also available dried and finely crushed. Can be used in almost every dish except desserts.	Tiny, mild, blue-black seeds that give a gentle flavor to sweet and savory dishes; sometimes crushed in a mortar and pestle to release juices for pastry fillings.	A pungent herb with leathery leaves. Often found fresh in bunches in late summer and early fall; more commonly found dried and crumbled. Use sparingly.	A fragrant and aromatic herb, mildly pungent, with tiny leaves. Often found fresh in pots; more frequently dried in leaf form or crumbled into powder. Use sparingly.
Borscht Gazpacho Mint Sauces for Lamb	Celery Soups Mushroom Soups Oyster Bisques Cream of Shrimp Soups	Beef and Tomato Bouillons Mushroom Soups Tomato Soups	Beef Soups Vegetable Soups	Creamed Vegetable Soups Fruit Soups Fish and Vegetable Butter Sauces	White Bean Soups Chicken and Turkey Soups Minestrones	Fish Chowders Beef Bouillons
Cucumber Salads Tomato Salads Melon Salads Mint-Yogurt Dressings	Chicken Salads Egg Salads Tomato Salads	Seafood Salads Mixed Vegetable Salads Orange and Grapefruit Vinaigrettes	Beef Salads Seafood Salads Cottage Cheese Salads Oil and Vinegar Dressings	Cottage Cheese Salads Fruit Salads Mayonnaise and Sour Cream Dressings	Turkey Salads Tongue or Ham Vinaigrettes	Ham Salads Turkey Salads Tuna Salads Mixed Vegetable Salads
Barbecued Lamb Roast Lamb Ground Meat Dishes	Hamburgers Meat Loaves Beef Stews Lamb and Veal Stuffings		Beef Pies, Pot Roasts and Stews Roast Meat Stuffings	Beef and Veal Stuffings Mustard Coatings for Roast Pork	Beef Roasts Pork Dishes Sausage Dishes Pork and Ham Stuffings	Roasts and Stews Meat Stuffings Variety Meat Dishes
Broiled Chicken Roast Duckling Roast Goose	Scrambled Eggs Omelets Soufflés Creamed Fish Dishes	Roast Chicken Broiled Shrimp Poultry and Fish Stuffings	Egg Dishes, especially Omelets Creamed Poultry Dishes Roast Poultry	Poached Whitefish Fish Stuffings	Roast Duck Roast Goose Poultry Stuffings	Deviled Eggs Chicken Turkey Duck Poultry Stuffings
Hot Cucumbers Summer Squash Tomatoes Zucchini	Green and Wax Beans Cabbage Corn Mashed Potatoes	Pasta Sauces Eggplant Mushrooms Onions Zucchini	Pasta Sauces Creamed Vegetable Sauces Vegetable Stuffings	Pasta Butter Sauces Cabbage New Potatoes Spinach Squash	Beets Celery Onions Squash	Beets Carrots Onions Potatoes
Poached Pears Pineapple Compotes	Coffee Cakes Fruit Pies Poached Fresh Fruits	Herb Breads	Toasted Herb Breads	Coffee Cakes Fruit Cakes Pastry Fillings Bread Toppings	Corn Breads Savory Bacon Biscuits Herb Breads	Corn Breads Herb Breads and Biscuits
Mint Teas Iced Fruit Juices	Iced Coffee and Tea Fruit Punches					Vegetable Juice Cocktails

LITTLE-COOK RECIPES

Most food must be cooked, if only for a short time. Here are some interesting and different recipes that use only the smallest amount of heat. Dissolving gelatin for Layered Cheese-Cranberry Salad takes merely a minute over the lowest of heat; crisping bacon for Chick Pea Mushroom Salad takes no more than 3 or 4 minutes; and Oyster Stew will be cooked and steaming hot in just 5 minutes.

No recipe requires more than 15 minutes of cooking time. While convenience foods and precooked ingredients are sometimes suggested to speed along the cooking process, wise purchases of fresh produce and fresh meat are also an important part of these little-cook recipes.

No matter how short the time you spend cooking, your meals will be elegant as well as easy if you remember these hints.

• Most fresh vegetables (frozen ones, too) are ready in less than 10 minutes; many are crisp-tender in under 5 minutes. Barely cooked asparagus or crunchy whole green beans are the perfect fresh accompaniments to Beef Stroganoff, Veal Scaloppine or Chinese Pork Fried Rice.

• Fresh boneless chicken breast, pounded thin and rolled to contain a filling, cooks in about 15 minutes. For a gala dinner, you can turn out

Chicken Bracciole in a jiffy.

• Fresh seafood cooks quickly, too—in fact, it is usually best if cooked for less than 10 minutes. Serve up some briefly cooked shrimp in a simple lemon-butter sauce, or spoon a mixture of butter, garlic, wine and bread crumbs over the shrimp and pop them in the oven for an aromatic Baked Shrimp, Scampi Style.

• Stir-fry recipes are ideal energy-savers. After the ingredients have been assembled and the meat and vegetables have been cut, shredded or minced, the actual cooking time for most Chinese-style main dishes is less than 8 minutes.

• For dessert, top-of-the-stove sauces can be prepared in just a few minutes to serve over heaping dishes of fresh fruit and ice cream. Try Vanilla Ice Cream with Hot Minced Topping—a mixture of mincemeat and cranberry relish, flamed in rum, then spooned over fresh pear chunks and ice cream.

If the oven or broiler is turned on, use this heat to cook or warm other dishes. If the top-of-the-stove burners are used, place other food alongside to warm from the same source of heat. And when planning menus, look for no-cook recipes to complement these little-cook ones.

Take advantage of these energy-saving recipes to trim your kitchen energy costs. These dishes are all little-cook—but they get big compliments.

MUSHROOM FLORENTINE

one 10-ounce package frozen chopped
   spinach, thawed
2 to 3 tablespoons cream cheese, softened
3 tablespoons butter or margarine
1 to 2 tablespoons horseradish
1 egg, beaten
12 to 15 large mushroom caps
   (reserve stems)
2 tablespoons water

MUSHROOM TOPPING
1 cup dry seasoned bread crumbs
1 tablespoon instant minced onion
2 tablespoons grated Parmesan cheese
1 egg, beaten
¼ cup chopped mushroom stems
12 to 15 tiny whole clams, drained
2 tablespoons butter or margarine
4 to 5 thin slices process cheese

1. Preheat oven to 400° F. In small saucepan, cover spinach with hot water, bring to boiling point and cook rapidly for 3 minutes. Drain and squeeze dry.

2. In a well-greased 9-inch pie plate, combine spinach with cream cheese, 1 tablespoon of the butter or margarine, the horseradish and 1 beaten egg. Mix well and spread out in an even layer; set aside.

3. In a large saucepan with tight-fitting cover, steam mushroom caps a few at a time with the remaining 2 tablespoons butter or margarine and 2 tablespoons water. Steam for 2 to 3 minutes, then drain on paper towels.

4. To make mushroom topping: In a small bowl, combine bread crumbs, minced onion, grated cheese, 1 beaten egg and ¼ cup chopped mushroom stems (reserved from mushroom caps). Fill caps with bread crumb mixture; top each cap with a drained clam. Dot 2 tablespoons butter or margarine over clams. Arrange filled mushrooms over spinach in pie plate.

5. Bake for 8 to 10 minutes. Cover top with slices of cheese and return to oven for another 5 minutes. Cut immediately through soft melted cheese into small wedges. *Serves 4 to 6.*

EnergySaving Tip: Since there are more one- and two-person families these days, the sales of small kitchen appliances, such as toaster ovens, continue to increase. Toaster ovens are particularly energy efficient; they require only 2 minutes to preheat and they can, in most instances, bake, toast and broil. Good to know are the sizes of dishes that easily fit into most toaster ovens.
- four to six 6-ounce individual custard cups.
- six 4-ounce individual soufflé dishes.
- two or three 10-ounce individual casserole dishes.
- one muffin pan for six 2½-inch muffins.
- one 9 x 5 x 3-inch loaf pan.

Microwave ovens are similar energy-savers. Each brand has its own specific cooking instructions; be sure to follow these instructions precisely. Whatever the brand, remember to place nothing that contains metal in a microwave. Glass, paper and ceramic cooking dishes are perfect. For maximum efficiency and the shortest possible cooking time, rotate the dishes in the oven a quarter or half turn from time to time. And for vegetables such as potatoes or squash, turn over every 2 to 3 minutes.

CHILLED CUCUMBER SOUP

½ cup raisins
½ cup boiling water
1 large cucumber
1 hard-cooked egg
2 tablespoons sliced green onion
2 cups unflavored yogurt
½ cup light cream
1 tablespoon dried parsley
1 teaspoon dill seed
1 teaspoon salt
¼ teaspoon pepper
1 cup seasoned croutons
½ cup chopped cucumber
lemon slices

1. In a small bowl, soak raisins in ½ cup boiling water for 5 minutes. Pare the cucumber and cut into 4 long wedges; remove seeds.

2. In electric blender, coarsely chop cucumber and hard-cooked egg. Transfer raisins to container with slotted spoon, reserving liquid. Add green onion and process on high for 30 seconds, or until smooth.

3. In a large glass or ceramic bowl, combine unflavored yogurt and light cream. Stir in cucumber mixture, parsley, dill seed, salt and pepper. Cover bowl with plastic wrap. (If soup seems too thick, thin with reserved raisin liquid.)

4. Chill for 2 to 3 hours to blend flavors. Ladle into chilled glass bowls and serve with croutons, ½ cup chopped cucumber and the lemon slices as garnish. *Serves 4.*

JELLIED TOMATO CONSOMME

1 envelope unflavored gelatin
¾ cup cold water
2 cups tomato juice
2 envelopes or cubes instant beef broth
1 tablespoon lemon juice
1 teaspoon Worcestershire sauce
¼ teaspoon pepper
sour cream
4 lemon slices

1. Sprinkle gelatin over ¼ cup of the cold water. Let stand for 5 minutes to soften.

2. In medium saucepan over moderate heat, bring the remaining ½ cup water, tomato juice, instant beef broth, lemon juice, Worcestershire sauce and pepper to boiling point. Lower heat and simmer for about 5 minutes. Stir in gelatin mixture and heat, stirring often, until gelatin dissolves.

3. Pour tomato mixture into a medium-size glass bowl. Chill 3 hours, or until set.

4. Spoon jellied tomato consommé into small soup bowls and garnish each with sour cream and a lemon slice. *Serves 4.*

TANGY TOMATO-CHEESE SOUP

one 10¾-ounce can condensed tomato
   soup
one 10¾-ounce can condensed Cheddar
   cheese soup
½ soup can evaporated milk
½ soup can milk
1 teaspoon Worcestershire sauce

½ teaspoon celery salt
¼ teaspoon cayenne pepper
3 slices bacon
2 tablespoons butter or margarine
½ teaspoon garlic powder
one 3-ounce can Chinese fried noodles

1. In a large saucepan, combine condensed tomato and condensed Cheddar cheese soup, evaporated milk, milk, Worcestershire sauce, celery salt and cayenne pepper until well blended; cook over medium heat, stirring often, until heated through.

2. Meanwhile, sauté bacon in a medium skillet over medium heat until almost crisp; drain on paper towels. Crumble bacon and add to soup; keep warm.

3. Wipe out skillet with paper towels. Melt butter or margarine in skillet over medium heat; stir in garlic powder, then fried noodles. Toss noodles in garlic butter until well coated. Continue cooking over medium heat, stirring all the time, until noodles are crisp and hot.

4. Ladle soup into bowls; top with garlic-flavored Chinese noodles. *Serves 4.*

SHRIMP CREOLE SOUP

2 tablespoons butter or margarine
one 6-ounce bag frozen shrimp, thawed
¼ teaspoon garlic powder
¼ teaspoon pepper
one 10¾-ounce can condensed tomato
   soup
one 10¾-ounce can condensed cream of
   shrimp soup

1 cup half-and-half or light cream
1 teaspoon instant minced onion
butter or margarine
4 large crisp crackers
¼ cup grated sharp Cheddar cheese

1. Melt butter or margarine in a large saucepan over medium heat; add shrimp and sauté. Stir in garlic powder and pepper.

2. Remove from heat, stir in condensed tomato and condensed cream of shrimp soup. Mix well and return to heat. Stir in half-and-half or light cream and minced onion. Bring almost to boiling point, stirring constantly.

3. Butter the crackers and sprinkle with cheese. Toast under broiler until cheese bubbles.

4. Pour soup into 4 bowls; top each with hot cheese cracker. Serve at once. *Serves 4.*

CHICKEN CORN CHOWDER

one 10¾-ounce can condensed cream of
  potato soup
one 10¾-ounce can condensed cream of
  chicken soup
one 16-ounce can cream-style corn

one 5-ounce can boneless chicken
1 cup milk
butter
pepper or paprika
tiny cheese crackers

1. In a large saucepan, combine condensed cream of potato and chicken soup, and corn. Break up chicken into chunks and add to saucepan. Slowly stir in milk.

2. Cook over medium heat, stirring often to prevent sticking, until mixture bubbles.

3. Ladle soup into heated bowls. Float pat of butter in center and lightly sprinkle with pepper or paprika. Serve with cheese crackers. *Serves 4.*

QUICK CLAM CHOWDER

2 slices bacon, diced
⅓ cup finely chopped onion
two 10¾-ounce cans condensed cream of
  potato soup

1 soup can half-and-half or evaporated
  milk
one 10-ounce can whole baby clams
oyster crackers

1. Sauté diced bacon in large saucepan over medium heat until crisp; remove with slotted spoon and drain on paper towels. Set aside.

2. Add onion and sauté in bacon fat until transparent, not brown. Lower heat.

3. Stir in condensed cream of potato soup, half-and-half or evaporated milk, and clams and their liquid; mix well. Cook over low heat, stirring often, for 10 minutes, or until soup is heated through and almost bubbles.

4. Ladle soup into heated bowls and sprinkle with reserved crumbled bacon. Serve with oyster crackers. *Serves 4.*

OYSTER STEW

1 pint oysters or two 8-ounce cans tiny
  oysters
1 teaspoon lemon juice
¼ cup butter or margarine
1 teaspoon Worcestershire sauce
½ cup crushed saltine crackers

1 cup light cream
1 cup milk
paprika
butter
saltine crackers

1. Drain liquor from oysters into a medium saucepan; add lemon juice and bring to boiling point. Add oysters and cook for 2 to 3 minutes, or until oysters curl. Set aside.

2. In another medium saucepan, melt butter or margarine; stir in Worcestershire sauce and crushed crackers until well blended.

3. Slowly add light cream and milk; warm through over low heat, stirring often. Add oysters and their liquid; heat thoroughly, but *do not boil*. Serve in heated soup crocks, topped with paprika and a small pat of butter. Serve with additional saltine crackers. *Serves 4.*

SPICED FRUIT SOUP

2 cups pineapple juice
2 cups water
one 6-ounce can frozen lemonade
  concentrate, thawed
¼ cup quick-cooking tapioca
¼ cup sugar
3 whole cloves

one 3-inch stick cinnamon
one 10-ounce package frozen sliced
  strawberries
2 medium eating oranges, peeled and
  sectioned
2 small bananas, peeled and sliced
sour cream

1. In a large saucepan, combine pineapple juice, water, thawed lemonade concentrate, tapioca, sugar, cloves and cinnamon stick. Let stand 10 minutes.

2. Bring to boiling over moderate heat. Lower heat and simmer for 5 minutes. Turn off heat and remove spices with slotted spoon.

3. Add frozen strawberries and stir until berries thaw. Add orange sections and banana slices. Ladle into soup bowls and top with a swirl of sour cream. Serve at room temperature, or chill until serving time. *Serves 8.*

ELLY'S LAYERED SALAD

1 cup shredded or finely sliced iceberg
   lettuce
1 cup finely sliced romaine lettuce
2 cups finely chopped celery
1 cup finely chopped green pepper
1 cup finely chopped red onion

one 8-ounce can peas, well drained
1 cup mayonnaise
½ cup grated Parmesan cheese
3 to 5 slices bacon, crisply cooked and
   crumbled

1. In a straight-sided glass bowl, layer iceberg, romaine, celery, green pepper, red onion and peas. Carefully spread mayonnaise over top, sealing surface. Sprinkle Parmesan cheese over mayonnaise; sprinkle crumbled bacon over cheese.

2. Cover bowl with plastic wrap. Chill at least 8 to 12 hours to blend flavors.

3. At serving time, *do not toss.* Scoop out servings with large fork and spoon, going straight down into bowl. *Serves 4 to 6.*

CHICK PEA MUSHROOM SALAD

one 20-ounce can chick peas
6 slices bacon
1 cup sliced fresh mushrooms
¼ cup lemon juice
½ cup thinly sliced red onion
1 small clove garlic, crushed

2 tablespoons chopped parsley
¼ teaspoon pepper
¼ cup vegetable oil
1 cup coarsely chopped tomatoes
1 cup seasoned croutons
lettuce cups

1. Rinse and drain chick peas; set aside. Fry bacon in a small skillet until crisp. Drain on paper towels, crumble and set aside. Pour off all but 2 tablespoons of fat from skillet. Add mushrooms and sauté in hot fat. Remove skillet from heat and stir in 1 tablespoon of the lemon juice.

2. In a large bowl, toss together the chick peas, crumbled bacon, sautéed mushrooms, red onion, garlic, parsley and pepper.

3. Combine remaining lemon juice and the oil; add to salad. Chill for 1 or 2 hours. Add tomatoes and croutons, toss lightly and serve at once in lettuce cups. *Serves 4.*

CRUNCHY CHICKEN SALAD

2 cups diced cooked chicken
one 4½-ounce can whole button
mushrooms, drained
3 slices bacon, crisply cooked and
crumbled
¾ cup diced carrots
¾ cup diced celery

½ cup quartered water chestnuts
1 tablespoon lemon juice
½ cup sour cream
½ cup mayonnaise
1 cup shredded lettuce
one 3-ounce can Chinese rice noodles

1. In large bowl, combine chicken, mushrooms, bacon, carrots, celery, water chestnuts and lemon juice until well blended. Cover with plastic wrap and chill 4 hours, or overnight, to blend flavors.

2. Just before serving, mix sour cream and mayonnaise in a small bowl; combine ¾ cup of this mixture with chicken-vegetable mixture.

3. Spread shredded lettuce over surface of shallow salad bowl. Add chicken salad and mix together gently, but thoroughly.

4. Heat noodles in 300° F oven for 3 or 4 minutes until crisp. Scatter half the noodles over salad in bowl. Serve with small bowls of remaining noodles and sour cream-mayonnaise mixture alongside. *Serves 4.*

TURKEY SALAD ORIENTALE

1½ cups diced cooked turkey
1 cup cooked rice
1 cup canned bean sprouts, drained (from
a 1-pound can)
⅔ cup chopped celery
⅔ cup finely chopped carrots
3 tablespoons bottled French dressing
2 tablespoons chopped parsley
1 tablespoon chopped green onion
⅛ teaspoon garlic powder

salt and pepper to taste
⅓ cup mayonnaise or salad dressing
lettuce leaves
one 3-ounce can Chinese fried noodles,
heated
2 slices bacon, crisply cooked and
crumbled
Cranberry-Cheese Crescent Rolls
(page 43)

1. In a large bowl, combine turkey, cooked rice, bean sprouts, celery, carrots, French dressing, parsley, green onion, garlic powder, salt and pepper; mix lightly until well blended. Cover with plastic wrap. Chill at least 2 hours to blend flavors.

2. Just before serving, gently fold in mayonnaise or salad dressing until well blended.

3. Line large serving platter with lettuce. Mound turkey salad over the lettuce. Garnish with crisp Chinese fried noodles and crumbled bacon. Serve with Cranberry-Cheese Crescent Rolls. *Serves 4. (Shown on page 50.)*

Note: Any cooked ham or poultry or leftover meat may be substituted for the turkey.

Cranberry-Cheese Crescent Rolls

one 8-ounce package refrigerator crescent rolls
one 3-ounce package cream cheese, at room temperature

one 14-ounce jar cranberry-orange relish, or one 8-ounce can whole berry cranberry sauce

1. Unroll crescent rolls; spread thinly with cream cheese.

2. Spread 1 teaspoon cranberry-orange relish or cranberry sauce over cream cheese.

3. Roll up crescents and bake according to label directions. *Serves 4. (Shown on page 50.)*

LAYERED CHEESE-CRANBERRY SALAD

2 envelopes unflavored gelatin
½ cup cold water
1¾ cups orange juice
1 cup heavy cream
one 3-ounce package cream cheese, softened
⅓ cup chopped walnuts
one 11-ounce can mandarin oranges, drained

one 16-ounce can whole berry cranberry sauce
¼ teaspoon ground allspice
⅛ teaspoon ground nutmeg (optional)
1 cup lemon-lime soda
1 tablespoon lemon juice (optional)
sour cream or mayonnaise (optional)

1. In a small saucepan, sprinkle one of the envelopes of gelatin over ¼ cup of the cold water; stir until gelatin softens. Heat, stirring constantly, until gelatin dissolves. Stir in orange juice. Chill until mixture is the consistency of unbeaten egg whites, about 30 minutes.

2. Using electric mixer at high speed, beat heavy cream in medium bowl until stiff; gently blend in softened cream cheese; add walnuts.

3. Fold cream cheese mixture into syrupy gelatin mixture; pour into a 9-inch square pan and chill until sticky-firm, about 45 minutes.

4. In small saucepan, sprinkle the remaining envelope gelatin over the remaining ¼ cup cold water; stir until gelatin softens. Heat, stirring constantly, until gelatin dissolves.

5. In medium bowl, combine drained mandarin oranges (reserve a few for garnish), whole berry cranberry sauce, allspice, nutmeg if used, lemon-lime soda, and lemon juice if used; add gelatin mixture and stir well. Chill until mixture is consistency of unbeaten egg whites.

6. Pour this syrupy mixture over sticky-firm layer in pan. Chill 4 hours, or overnight.

7. To serve, cut into 6 to 8 squares; lift out with a pancake turner. Top with sour cream or mayonnaise, if desired. Garnish with reserved mandarin oranges. *Serves 6 to 8.*

BARBECUED HAMBURGER

½ cup finely chopped onion
2 tablespoons vegetable oil
1½ pounds ground chuck
¼ cup ketchup
¼ cup bottled barbecue sauce
¼ cup tomato paste
2 tablespoons vinegar
1 tablespoon brown sugar
1 tablespoon prepared mustard
1 teaspoon hot pepper sauce

½ teaspoon ground cloves
¼ teaspoon garlic powder
salt and pepper to taste
4 to 6 hard rolls, warmed
shredded lettuce
tomato slices
pickle slices
Muenster or Monterey Jack cheese, cut
   into strips

1. Sauté onion in oil in large skillet over medium heat until lightly browned; add ground chuck in one large patty. Brown and break up ground chuck while cooking it for about 5 minutes. Drain off surplus oil.

2. In medium bowl, combine ketchup, barbecue sauce, tomato paste, vinegar, brown sugar, mustard, hot pepper sauce, cloves, garlic powder, salt and pepper; mix well. Add to ground chuck-onion mixture in skillet; mix well.

3. Simmer over low heat, stirring occasionally, for 15 to 20 minutes, or until mixture is hot and flavors are well blended.

4. Split hard rolls; divide meat mixture between rolls. Serve with shredded lettuce, tomato slices, pickle slices and cheese strips. *Serves 4.*

PHILADELPHIA HOAGIES

1½ pounds boneless beef chuck steak
2 tablespoons butter or margarine
2 cups shredded American process cheese
6 hero rolls, split and warmed
¾ cup chopped red onion
2 cups chopped iceberg lettuce

1½ cups thinly sliced tomatoes
1 cup cooked sliced mushrooms
ketchup
chili sauce
hot pepper sauce

1. Place chuck steak in freezer for 15 minutes or until firm. Cut into very thin slices.

2. Melt butter or margarine in large skillet over moderate heat. Brown half of the beef slices on one side. With tongs, turn beef and sprinkle with half the shredded cheese. Cover skillet and cook 1 to 2 minutes.

3. Pile beef-cheese mixture into 3 hero rolls and keep warm while preparing remaining beef and cheese.

4. When all 6 hero rolls are filled, sprinkle beef with chopped red onion. Pass chopped lettuce, sliced tomatoes and mushrooms, ketchup, chili sauce and hot pepper sauce to pile on beef as desired. *Serves 6.*

FAKE "STEAK"

1½ pounds ground chuck
2 large eggs
1½ teaspoons salt
¼ teaspoon pepper
¼ teaspoon garlic powder
2 tablespoons butter or margarine
1 cup thin sliced onion rings
1 green pepper, halved, seeded and cut
   into chunks

one 4½-ounce can mushrooms, drained
   (reserve liquid)
2 tablespoons flour
2 teaspoons liquid gravy seasoning
2 tablespoons Worcestershire or
   steak sauce

1. In a medium bowl, combine ground chuck, eggs, salt, pepper and garlic powder, mixing just until blended.

2. On waxed paper, shape meat with a fork and spoon into a T-bone steak shape (at least 1 inch thick). Cover with waxed paper. Chill at least 15 minutes to firm up.

3. Meanwhile, melt butter or margarine in a medium skillet over medium heat; add onion rings, green pepper and drained mushrooms and sauté for 3 to 5 minutes, or until soft; stir in flour and liquid gravy seasoning; slowly add reserved mushroom liquid and enough water to measure 1 cup, stirring constantly. Lower heat and simmer, stirring often, for 15 minutes, or until mixture thickens; add more water if sauce is too thick.

4. Preheat broiler. Remove top sheet of waxed paper from "steak" and flip steak over onto broiling pan; brush top with Worcestershire or steak sauce.

5. Broil 5 inches from heat, 2 to 4 minutes per side. (For well done, turn off heat after broiling; let steak set an additional 2 to 3 minutes before removing from broiler.)

6. Slice steak thickly. Serve with onion-pepper-mushroom sauce. *Serves 4.*

EnergySaving Tip: Cooking for a short period of time with intense heat is the oldest, most efficient way of utilizing precious energy. The Chinese instinctively knew this when they stir-fried their foods. Broiling and frying are but an extension of the concept of cooking with short, sharp, bursts of energy. For optimum success, follow these rules:
• Broil foods quickly on both sides to seal in juices; then, turn to the original side to cook longer; turn once more to finish cooking.
• When frying, whether shallow or deep-fat frying, make sure the oil is hot. The surface of the oil should shimmer and there should be a faint haze above the oil; hot oil should not smoke. If you have a deep-fat thermometer, heat the oil until the thermometer registers between 325° and 350° F.
• All food that is fried should first be coated with flour or egg and bread crumbs. If frying a thick cut of veal or other meat, coat with flour, then dip in beaten egg and coat with bread crumbs. Very thin cuts of meat such as pounded veal and chicken breasts, which are cooked in little oil, need only the thinnest flour coating.
• Thicker foods, such as chicken cooked in deeper fat, need heavier egg and bread crumb coating. Chill all coated foods before cooking to firmly set the coating. This will also make the food crisp, by sealing in the juices immediately.

TACOS PRONTO

2 brown-and-serve pork sausages, finely
  chopped
½ cup finely chopped onion
1¼ pounds ground beef
¼ very small chili pepper, dried and
  crushed, or 1 tablespoon chili powder
½ teaspoon cumin powder
¼ teaspoon garlic powder

salt and pepper to taste
one 6-ounce can tomato paste
½ cup dry red wine
8 corn tortillas
1 cup shredded lettuce
1 cup shredded Monterey Jack or Cheddar
  cheese
2 tomatoes, coarsely chopped

1. In large skillet over medium heat, sauté chopped sausages until crisp, about 5 minutes; remove from skillet and set aside. Sauté onion in pan drippings until golden; remove and set aside. Shape ground beef into a large patty in skillet; brown 5 minutes on each side, then break up into small chunks. Return chopped sausages and onion to skillet; mix well.

2. Stir in crushed chili pepper or chili powder, cumin powder, garlic powder, salt and pepper; mix well. In a small bowl, mix tomato paste and wine; stir into skillet. Simmer mixture over low heat for 5 minutes. (If too thick, add more wine and some water.)

3. Lightly sauté corn tortillas on a hot greased griddle or in a large skillet until slightly crisp; fold. Fill tacos with beef mixture and serve immediately. Top with shredded lettuce, shredded cheese and chopped tomatoes, passed separately in small bowls. *Serves 4.*

BEEF STROGANOFF

1 pound beef tenderloin
flour
1 pound fresh mushrooms
1 cup butter or margarine
¼ cup chopped onion

¼ cup dry white wine (optional)
1 cup sour cream
salt and pepper to taste
cooked rice

1. Place meat in freezer for 30 minutes to firm up; cut into narrow strips and dust with flour. Wipe mushrooms with a damp cloth; slice thinly and set aside.

2. Melt half of the butter or margarine in large heavy skillet over medium heat; add beef strips and sauté, turning often, for 3 minutes, or until cooked but still slightly pink inside. Remove beef from skillet and keep warm.

3. Melt remaining butter or margarine in skillet; add onion and sauté until slightly transparent, but not brown. Add mushrooms and cover skillet; cook for 2 to 3 minutes, stirring once or twice, until mushrooms are soft. (If there is not enough moisture in skillet, add white wine.)

4. Return beef strips to skillet, carefully mixing with onion and mushrooms; cook over low heat for 1 to 2 minutes. Stir in sour cream, salt and pepper; cook over low heat for 2 to 3 minutes, or until heated through. *Do not boil.* Serve with long-grain and wild rice mixture or with plain buttered rice. *Serves 4.*

VEAL SCALOPPINE

1 pound boneless veal slices, from leg or shoulder	**Seasoned Bread Crumbs (below)**
¼ cup flour	**2 tablespoons vegetable oil**
1 egg	**2 tablespoons butter or margarine**
1 tablespoon water	**one 6-ounce package sliced mozzarella cheese**

1. Place veal slices between sheets of waxed paper and pound with a heavy knife or smooth side of wooden mallet until very thin.

2. On waxed paper, coat veal slices with flour. In a pie plate, beat egg and water until smooth. Prepare Seasoned Bread Crumbs and sprinkle on another sheet of waxed paper. Dip floured veal into beaten egg, then into bread crumbs to coat completely.

3. Arrange coated veal slices on a cookie sheet; chill at least 20 minutes. (Cover with plastic wrap if prepared well ahead of time.)

4. Heat oil and butter or margarine in a large skillet. Brown veal, a few slices at a time, 2 to 3 minutes per side.

5. Arrange cooked veal in a flameproof 13 x 9 x 2-inch casserole. Top with cheese slices. Broil 2 minutes, or until cheese melts. Serve immediately. *Serves 4.*

Seasoned Bread Crumbs

3 slices day-old bread	**½ teaspoon oregano**
2 tablespoons grated Parmesan cheese	**½ teaspoon salt**
1 tablespoon dried parsley	**¼ teaspoon pepper**

1. Break up bread into container of an electric blender. Add grated cheese, parsley, oregano, salt and pepper.

2. Cover and process on high for 30 seconds, or until smooth. (Crumbs may be made ahead and stored in a screwtop jar in refrigerator.)

EnergySaving Tip: Even a quick skillet beef stroganoff, made with a luxury-item beef tenderloin, can be turned into a double energy-saver. Just make double the quantity in a very large skillet, or even in a deep Dutch oven; remove half of the double recipe for freezing (do not add sour cream to this do-ahead part). Another tip for saving energy: The thinner that meat is cut or pounded, the quicker it will cook. Freezing meat slightly before slicing with a very sharp knife will make this cutting process easier. Pounding veal between two sheets of foil or plastic wrap is easier than pounding between sheets of waxed paper; use only the flat side of a wooden mallet.

CHINESE PORK FRIED RICE

3 tablespoons butter or margarine
1 cup chopped onion
1 cup fresh bean sprouts
4 cups cooked rice
2 cups finely diced roasted pork

2 tablespoons soy sauce
2 tablespoons chopped parsley
1½ teaspoons salt
½ teaspoon pepper
2 eggs, lightly beaten

1. Melt butter or margarine in large skillet over medium heat; add onion and sauté for 2 minutes, or until lightly browned. Add bean sprouts and sauté for 1 to 2 minutes. Add cooked rice and sauté for 2 to 3 minutes longer.

2. Mix in pork, soy sauce, parsley, salt and pepper; continue cooking for 2 to 3 minutes, stirring often; push mixture to side of skillet.

3. Pour lightly beaten eggs into center of skillet; cook, stirring several times, until slightly scrambled. Break up eggs with fork and mix in pork and vegetables.

4. Cook for 2 minutes longer. Remove from heat and cover skillet. Let stand 2 minutes to steam. Uncover and serve. *Serves 4.*

HAM AND BROCCOLI ROLL-UPS

two 10-ounce packages frozen broccoli, thawed
8 to 10 slices boiled ham (slightly thicker slices than for sandwiches)

8 to 10 thin slices cheese (Swiss, American or other packaged cheese)
two ¾-ounce packages hollandaise sauce mix

1. Preheat oven to 375° F. Cook broccoli according to label directions until tender; drain.

2. Spread ham slices on a flat surface. Top each ham slice with a slice of cheese. Place a cooked broccoli floweret at either end of ham and cheese slice; roll up so broccoli flowerets project from both ends.

3. Place roll-ups on heatproof serving platter. Bake 5 to 8 minutes until heated through. Cheese should be just slightly melted.

4. Make hollandaise sauce mix according to label directions to make 1 cup. Pour about ½ cup sauce over roll-ups. Pass extra sauce. *Serves 4.*

Avocado Crab Louis (page 21)

Turkey Salad Orientale with Cranberry-Cheese Crescent Rolls (pages 42 and 43)

Baked Shrimp, Scampi Style (page 56)

Lamb and Fruit Skewers (page 78)

HAM HASH OMELET

2 tablespoons vegetable oil
1 cup finely chopped cooked ham
1 cup chopped boiled potatoes
½ cup chopped cooked carrots
½ cup chopped onion

2 tablespoons chopped parsley
3 large eggs
½ cup milk
⅛ teaspoon pepper

1. Heat oil in a large heavy skillet. Stir in ham, potatoes, carrots, onion and parsley. Cook and stir over moderate heat for about 5 minutes.

2. In a small bowl, beat together eggs, milk and pepper. Pour over sizzling ham mixture. (Quickly tilt pan to even out egg layer.)

3. Cover and cook for 4 to 5 minutes. Uncover and quickly brown under broiler.

4. Divide into 4 wedges to serve. *Serves 4.*

Note: This is a delicious way to use up leftovers.

BAKED SWISS HAM AND EGGS

4 thin slices cooked ham
4 thin slices Swiss cheese
½ cup heavy cream
4 eggs

½ cup chopped cooked ham
1 teaspoon mild paprika
4 English muffins, split, toasted and
    buttered

1. Preheat oven to 400° F.

2. Grease a heatproof 8 x 12 x 2-inch baking dish; cover bottom with sliced ham, then cheese. Pour half of the heavy cream over ham and cheese in dish. Carefully break eggs into dish, one over each pile of ham and cheese; sprinkle chopped ham around eggs. Pour remaining cream over eggs and sprinkle with paprika.

3. Bake for 10 to 15 minutes, or until eggs are set.

4. Place muffins on serving plates; carefully spoon 1 egg (and the ham and cheese underneath) over each muffin. Serve immediately. *Serves 4 to 6.*

FRENCH HAM SANDWICH

8 thin slices wide country-style white
  bread (or your favorite bread,
  thinly sliced)
1 tablespoon butter or margarine, at room
  temperature
¼ cup mayonnaise or salad dressing
½ pound thickly sliced cooked ham
  (about 5 or 6 slices)

¼ pound sliced Swiss cheese
  (about 6 or 7 slices)
3 eggs
3 tablespoons milk, heavy cream or
  evaporated milk
1 teaspoon salt
¼ teaspoon pepper

1. Spread 4 slices bread with butter or margarine; spread remaining 4 slices bread with 1 tablespoon of the mayonnaise or salad dressing.

2. Cutting ham and cheese to fit within bread, top each buttered bread slice with alternate layers of ham, Swiss cheese, remaining mayonnaise or salad dressing, ham and Swiss cheese. Top with remaining bread slices, mayonnaise side down.

3. Beat eggs in pie plate until frothy; beat in milk, cream or evaporated milk; add salt and pepper. Carefully dip each sandwich into beaten egg mixture, covering both sides.

4. Preheat nonstick griddle, sandwich grill or large skillet to medium; add butter, if necessary. Sauté sandwiches, turning once, for 5 to 7 minutes, or until both sides are golden brown and sandwiches are heated through with the cheese slightly melted.

5. Slice sandwiches in half. Serve immediately with dill pickles, potato chips and applesauce. *Serves 4.*

HOT DOG ROLL-UPS

three 8-ounce packages refrigerator
  biscuits
butter or margarine, softened

⅔ cup shredded sharp Cheddar cheese
10 frankfurters
assorted condiments

1. Preheat oven to 375° F. Place 3 biscuits end to end on floured board; press dough together. Roll into a rectangle large enough to wrap around a frankfurter; spread dough with soft butter or margarine.

2. Sprinkle 1 tablespoon shredded cheese over dough, top with 3 or 4 favorite condiments (a teaspoon each of sweet pickle relish, chopped onion and taco sauce, for example).

3. Place frankfurter on top of condiments. Bring dough up and around frankfurter, pinching dough together and sealing ends. Repeat this with remaining biscuits and frankfurters, varying the condiments with each one.

4. Place roll-ups on cookie sheet and bake for 12 to 15 minutes, or until golden brown. *Serves 4.*

CHEESE TACO DOGS

½ cup tomato sauce
¼ cup bottled taco sauce
dash hot pepper sauce (optional)
¼ cup water
1 teaspoon crumbled oregano

salt and pepper to taste
4 frankfurters
4 corn tortillas
1 cup shredded Monterey Jack or
    mozzarella cheese

1. In a small saucepan, combine tomato sauce, taco sauce (if taco sauce is mild, add hot pepper sauce), water, oregano, salt and pepper; cook over low heat for 10 minutes, or until mixture bubbles.

2. Place frankfurters and tortillas on a griddle or in a large skillet over medium heat. (If using a skillet, you may have to work in batches.) Spread each tortilla with 2 to 3 tablespoons of the tomato mixture; sprinkle with 2 to 3 tablespoons cheese. As cheese begins to melt and tortilla becomes crisp, place warmed frankfurter at one end of tortilla; roll up.

3. Cook 2 to 3 minutes longer. *Serves 4.*

Note: Refried beans, sauerkraut and other condiments of your choice may be placed on tortilla before adding frankfurter.

CHICKEN BRACCIOLE

4 whole chicken breasts, boned and
    halved
flour
8 thin slices cooked ham
8 thin slices cheese (such as Cheddar or
    Gruyère)
1 teaspoon salt

¼ teaspoon pepper
1 teaspoon garlic powder
¼ cup chopped parsley
1 egg, well beaten
¼ cup dry red wine
¼ cup butter, margarine or vegetable oil

1. Cover chicken breast halves with waxed paper or plastic wrap; pound gently until flattened and thinned. Lightly dredge with flour.

2. Place a ham slice, then a cheese slice, on each piece of chicken; sprinkle lightly with salt and pepper, garlic powder and chopped parsley. Roll up chicken breast halves, tucking in sides; secure with wooden toothpicks.

3. Dip chicken rolls in beaten egg, then wine, then beaten egg again. Melt butter, margarine or oil in a large skillet over medium-high heat; add chicken rolls. Cover skillet and cook chicken for 5 minutes; reduce heat to medium, uncover skillet and gently turn chicken rolls, browning on all sides. Continue cooking for 10 to 15 minutes longer.

4. Remove chicken rolls to a heated platter; remove toothpicks and serve immediately. *Serves 4.*

Note: For a crisper finish, cook chicken rolls in an uncovered skillet for a total of 20 minutes.

TURKEY 'N' BISCUITS

one 10¾-ounce can condensed cream of
   celery soup
¼ cup water or chicken broth
3 tablespoons butter or margarine
3 tablespoons dry sherry
2 cups diced cooked turkey

one 8-ounce can baby peas, drained
one 4-ounce can chopped mushrooms
¼ cup sour cream
one 8-ounce package refrigerator
   buttermilk biscuits, baked

1. In large saucepan, combine condensed cream of celery soup, water or chicken broth, 2 tablespoons of the butter or margarine, and 2 tablespoons of the sherry until well blended. Cook over low heat, stirring often, until hot.

2. Gently stir in turkey and drained peas. Continue cooking over low heat until turkey and peas are heated through.

3. Meanwhile, melt the remaining tablespoon butter or margarine in a small skillet. Add chopped mushrooms and sauté for 4 minutes, until just tender. Stir in remaining tablespoon of sherry and heat through.

4. Fold sour cream into hot turkey mixture. Serve immediately over buttermilk biscuits; top with mushrooms. *Serves 4.*

Note: Two cups diced cooked chicken or two 5-ounce cans boneless chicken may be substituted for the turkey in this recipe.

BAKED SHRIMP, SCAMPI STYLE

2 pounds medium shrimp, cooked, peeled
   and deveined
⅔ cup butter or margarine
2 small cloves garlic, crushed
¼ cup dry white wine

2 tablespoons chopped parsley
1 teaspoon lemon juice
1½ cups soft bread crumbs
1 teaspoon paprika

1. Preheat oven to 350° F, or preheat broiler. Drain cooked shrimp and place in a heavily greased, heatproof 13 x 9 x 2-inch dish.

2. Melt ½ cup of the butter or margarine in medium saucepan; add garlic and simmer over low heat for 2 minutes, or just until tender. Stir in wine, parsley and lemon juice; remove from heat. Mix in bread crumbs. Spoon mixture over shrimp in dish.

3. Cut remaining butter or margarine into small chunks; dot over shrimp mixture; sprinkle paprika over all.

4. Bake for about 15 minutes, or broil 4 inches from heat for 5 minutes, until mixture is heated through and golden brown. Serve immediately. *Serves 4. (Shown on page 51.)*

BROCCOLI AND SHRIMP BAKE

one 10-ounce package frozen broccoli
one 10¾-ounce can condensed cream of
    shrimp soup
¼ cup evaporated milk
¼ cup mayonnaise or salad dressing
¼ cup dry sherry
one 8-ounce package frozen cooked
    shrimp, thawed and well drained

2 teaspoons lemon juice
1 teaspoon salt
¼ teaspoon pepper
¼ teaspoon garlic powder
2 tablespoons butter or margarine
½ cup shredded cheese
2 tablespoons dry bread crumbs

1. In medium saucepan over medium heat, cook broccoli according to label directions for 5 minutes, or until barely tender; drain in colander.

2. In same saucepan, combine condensed cream of shrimp soup, evaporated milk, mayonnaise or salad dressing, and sherry until well blended. Cook over medium heat, stirring often, until heated through; add cooked shrimp.

3. Preheat broiler. Place drained broccoli in well-greased 9-inch glass pie dish; sprinkle with lemon juice, salt, pepper and garlic powder; dot with butter or margarine.

4. Spoon shrimp mixture over broccoli. In a small bowl, mix shredded cheese and bread crumbs; sprinkle over shrimp mixture.

5. Broil 5 inches from heat for 8 minutes, or until mixture is hot and bubbly and cheese topping is golden brown. *Serves 4.*

TUNA CHEESE PIE CASSEROLE

2 cups cooked rice
3 eggs
2 cups shredded or grated sharp Cheddar
    cheese

one 7-ounce can tuna, drained and flaked
¾ cup light cream or evaporated milk
salt and pepper to taste
paprika

1. Preheat oven to 400° F. Thoroughly mix cooked rice and 1 of the eggs, beaten. Press mixture on bottom and sides of greased 9-inch pie plate to form a crust.

2. Spread 1 cup of the grated cheese over rice. Spread flaked tuna over cheese. Top tuna with remaining cup of cheese.

3. In a small bowl, mix together light cream or evaporated milk, the 2 remaining eggs, salt and pepper. Pour over top layer of cheese; sprinkle with paprika.

4. Bake about 20 minutes until hot and bubbly. *Serves 4.*

Note: For variation, add ½ cup sautéed onion or celery, crisp crumbled bacon, or chopped nuts to the cream-egg mixture.

NOODLES WITH BUTTER

1 cup butter, at room temperature
1 cup freshly grated Parmesan cheese

½ cup heavy cream
one 16-ounce package fettuccine

1. Cream ⅔ cup of the butter in a heavy bowl with a large spoon; gradually beat in ⅔ cup of the cheese alternately with ¼ cup of the heavy cream; continue beating until mixture is light and fluffy.

2. Cook noodles in a large saucepan according to label directions for 7 to 9 minutes, or until tender but still chewy (al dente); drain very well in colander.

3. Place remaining ⅓ cup butter in same saucepan; return drained noodles to pan; toss gently over very low heat, until butter is melted and noodles are evenly coated.

4. Gradually add whipped butter-cheese mixture, tossing gently over very low heat; add remaining ¼ cup cream, then remaining ⅓ cup cheese. Toss gently and serve immediately with a green salad. *Serves 4 to 6 generously.*

Note: This is one of the very few recipes where *only* butter is really recommended.

LINGUINE WITH CLAM SAUCE

4 quarts water
1 tablespoon salt
one 16-ounce package linguine
1 tablespoon olive oil
1 tablespoon butter or margarine

3 cloves garlic, slivered
one 6½-ounce can minced clams
one 7¾-ounce can white clam sauce
chopped parsley
grated Parmesan cheese

1. Bring 4 quarts water to boiling point in a large kettle. Stir in salt. Add linguine, a handful at a time.

2. Cook linguine according to label directions until tender, about 10 minutes. Drain and keep warm.

3. Combine and heat olive oil and butter or margarine in a small saucepan. Add garlic and simmer for 5 minutes. Remove garlic.

4. Add minced clams (along with their liquid) and white clam sauce. Heat through for about 3 to 4 minutes.

5. To serve, heap warm linguine on warm platter. Pour sauce over linguine, sprinkle with chopped parsley and grated cheese. *Serves 4 to 6.*

RUMMY BANANAS

¼ cup butter or margarine
¼ cup brown sugar, firmly packed
1 tablespoon lemon juice

4 bananas, peeled and halved lengthwise
¼ cup light rum

1. Melt butter or margarine in a large heavy skillet or chafing dish over low heat; stir in brown sugar and lemon juice. Simmer, stirring often, for 5 minutes, or until mixture bubbles and thickens slightly.

2. Add banana halves, rounded side down; turn carefully to coat all sides with syrup. Simmer gently for about 1 minute.

3. Heat rum in a small saucepan over low heat; *do not boil.* Pour over bananas and carefully ignite, using a long match; baste until flames subside.

4. Remove skillet from heat. Carefully transfer bananas to 4 serving plates, spooning some sauce over each. Serve immediately. *Serves 4.*

PERSIAN COMPOTE

one 11-ounce package dried mixed fruit
1½ cups dried apple slices, cut into
   bite-size pieces
2 cups apple juice
½ cup water

1 teaspoon vanilla extract
½ cup heavy cream
1 tablespoon sugar
1 teaspoon grated lemon rind

1. Combine dried mixed fruit and dried apple pieces in a large saucepan. Pour in apple juice and water.

2. Bring to boiling point over high heat; lower heat and cover saucepan. Simmer for 10 minutes. Add vanilla extract and cool 1 hour in saucepan.

3. Pour fruit and apple juice mixture into a large glass or ceramic bowl. Cover bowl with plastic wrap and chill for 2 hours.

4. Using electric hand beater, beat heavy cream and sugar in a small deep bowl until stiff. Spoon fruit into dessert dishes with a slotted spoon; top with stiffly beaten heavy cream and sprinkle with lemon rind. *Serves 4.*

FRUIT CASSEROLE

two 16-ounce cans cherry pie filling
one 20-ounce can pineapple slices,
   drained
one 16-ounce can pear halves, drained

2 tablespoons brown sugar
¼ cup light rum
sour cream, light cream or ice cream

1. Preheat oven to 450° F, or preheat broiler.

2. Spread cherry pie filling over bottom of a well-greased 13 x 9 x 2-inch baking dish. Place pineapple slices over filling; fit a pear half rounded side up over each pineapple slice.

3. Sprinkle brown sugar over pears; pour rum over pineapple slices and cherry pie filling.

4. Bake for 10 minutes, or broil 4 inches from heat for 4 minutes, until brown sugar melts and dessert is hot. Serve with sour cream, light cream or ice cream. *Serves 6.*

LEMON WHIP

1 envelope unflavored gelatin
½ cup cold water
4 eggs, separated
1 cup sugar
⅓ cup freshly squeezed lemon juice

½ teaspoon salt
1½ tablespoons grated lemon rind
½ cup heavy cream
grated lemon rind or thinly sliced lemon
   (optional)

1. Soften gelatin in ½ cup cold water. Meanwhile, combine egg yolks, ½ cup of the sugar, lemon juice and salt in top of double boiler. Place over simmering (not boiling) water; cook, stirring often, until mixture thickens. Remove from heat.

2. Add softened gelatin mixture and 1½ tablespoons grated lemon rind; stir until gelatin dissolves. Cool.

3. Using electric mixer at high speed, beat egg whites in large bowl until they are frothy and hold soft peaks; gradually add the remaining ½ cup sugar, a tablespoon at a time. Beat until meringue is stiff and shiny. Gradually fold meringue into the cooled and slightly thickened lemon mixture.

4. Beat heavy cream in small bowl until soft peaks form; fold into lemon-meringue mixture. Pour into a 2-quart serving bowl. Cover with plastic wrap and chill 2 to 3 hours until firm.

5. To serve, spoon mixture into small bowls or dessert dishes; top with additional grated lemon rind or thinly sliced lemon, if desired. *Serves 4.*

CHERRY BRULEE

3 cups milk	**1 tablespoon butter or margarine**
½ cup farina	**1 teaspoon lemon rind**
¼ cup sugar	**one 20-ounce can cherry pie filling**
1 egg, separated	**2 tablespoons brown sugar**

1. Scald milk in a large saucepan over moderate heat. Sprinkle farina over milk and stir until well blended. Lower heat and simmer for 5 to 10 minutes. Remove from heat.

2. Add sugar, egg yolk, butter or margarine, and lemon rind; stir to blend. Return saucepan to heat and simmer for 2 to 3 minutes; cool. Beat egg white in a small bowl until stiff. Fold into slightly cooled mixture.

3. Preheat broiler. Heat cherry pie filling in a medium saucepan. Pour half the farina mixture into 1½-quart flameproof casserole. Top with heated cherry pie filling and cover with remaining farina mixture. Sprinkle with brown sugar.

4. Broil for 2 to 3 minutes, or until top is golden; serve warm. *Serves 6 to 8.*

HAWAIIAN FRUIT PIE

1½ cups graham cracker crumbs	**one 16-ounce container frozen**
¼ cup butter or margarine, melted	**dessert topping, thawed**
2 tablespoons sugar	**1 large banana**
two 8-ounce containers Hawaiian-style	**one 8-ounce can mandarin oranges,**
fruit salad yogurt	**drained**

1. Preheat oven to 375° F. In a medium bowl, use a fork to toss graham cracker crumbs with melted butter or margarine and sugar until well blended. Pat mixture into a 9-inch pie plate to make a smooth crust.

2. Bake for 7 minutes, or until firm. Cool completely on a wire rack.

3. In a medium bowl, combine fruit salad yogurt and ½ container of whipped topping. Spoon half of this mixture into cooled crust.

4. Slice half of banana over yogurt layer and arrange mandarin oranges around banana slices. (Reserve a few of the oranges for garnish, along with other half of banana.) Spread evenly with remaining yogurt mixture.

5. Freeze for 30 to 60 minutes, or until serving time. Decorate pie with spoonfuls of remaining ½ container of whipped topping and reserved banana and mandarin oranges. Cut and serve while still frozen. *Serves 8.*

Note: If frozen for several hours, let stand 5 minutes at room temperature before cutting.

PUMPKIN CHIFFON PIE

1½ cups gingersnap crumbs
   (about 20 gingersnaps)
⅓ cup butter or margarine, melted
1½ cups canned or cooked pumpkin
4 eggs, separated
1 cup evaporated milk
½ cup light brown sugar, firmly packed
1 teaspoon ground cinnamon
½ teaspoon ground ginger

½ teaspoon ground nutmeg
½ teaspoon ground allspice
½ teaspoon salt
1 envelope unflavored gelatin
¼ cup cold water
½ cup sugar
stiffly beaten heavy cream or refrigerator
   dessert topping
nutmeg (optional)

1. Preheat oven to 375° F. In a small bowl, mix gingersnap crumbs and melted butter or margarine. Press crumbs on bottom and sides of a 9-inch pie plate. Bake for 5 minutes; cool.

2. In top of double boiler over boiling water, stir pumpkin until heated through. Lower heat to a simmer.

3. In medium bowl, thoroughly mix egg yolks, evaporated milk, brown sugar, cinnamon, ginger, nutmeg, allspice and salt; add to pumpkin. Cook over hot water, stirring constantly, for about 12 minutes, or until mixture thickens and coats a metal spoon.

4. In a small saucepan, soften gelatin in ¼ cup cold water. Stir over low heat until gelatin dissolves; cool slightly. Stir gelatin mixture into pumpkin mixture. Chill until mixture thickens to consistency of unbeaten egg whites, about 45 minutes to 1 hour.

5. Using electric mixer at high speed, beat egg whites in medium bowl until foamy and double in volume. Add sugar, 1 tablespoon at a time, beating until soft peaks form. Fold meringue into the pumpkin mixture, then pour into cooled crust. Chill for at least 4 hours, or overnight.

6. When ready to serve, top pie with swirls of whipped cream or whipped topping. Sprinkle lightly with nutmeg, if desired. *Serves 6.*

Note: Pie may be frozen.

EnergySaving Tip: No-bake crumb crusts are the best way of saving expensive oven energy and baking time. The gingersnap crumb crust for Pumpkin Chiffon Pie (above) is baked, but could easily be chilled instead. Any crisp, sweetened cookie can be rolled into crumbs, tossed with melted butter or margarine, and then pressed evenly into a 9-inch pie plate; freeze for 10 minutes or refrigerate for 30 minutes, rather than baking. Always keep the proportions the same: 1½ cups crumbs to ⅓ cup butter or margarine, melted. If the crumbs are unsweetened, add ¼ to ⅓ cup granulated or brown sugar before tossing with melted butter or margarine. Try the following crust variations for any cool refrigerator or freezer dessert:
- Graham cracker crumbs, brown sugar and ¼ teaspoon cinnamon
- Chocolate wafer crumbs and ¼ teaspoon peppermint extract
- 1¼ cups vanilla wafer crumbs and ¼ cup finely chopped walnuts
- ¾ cup shortbread crumbs, ¾ cup finely chopped almonds and ¼ teaspoon almond extract

SILKY FRENCH PIE

½ cup unsalted butter, softened
⅔ cup sugar
one 1-ounce square unsweetened
   chocolate, melted and cooled
½ teaspoon vanilla extract

½ teaspoon rum extract
2 eggs
one 9-inch pie shell, baked and cooled
1 cup heavy cream, stiffly beaten
grated chocolate

1. Using electric mixer at high speed, cream butter in medium bowl until light and fluffy; gradually add sugar, beating well after each addition.

2. Beat melted and cooled chocolate into creamed butter mixture; add vanilla extract and rum extract. Beat in eggs, one at a time, beating a full 5 minutes after each addition (this is very important).

3. Pour mixture into cooled pie shell. Chill for 4 hours, or overnight. Just before serving, top pie with stiffly beaten heavy cream and grated chocolate. *Serves 6.*

Note: Use only butter and very fresh eggs. Follow directions carefully.

ESPRESSO MOUSSE

1 envelope unflavored gelatin
¼ cup cold water
½ cup brewed espresso coffee
½ cup sugar
1 egg white

1 cup heavy cream
⅓ cup chopped almonds
2 tablespoons Marsala wine
½ teaspoon grated lemon rind

1. Sprinkle gelatin over ¼ cup cold water. Let stand for 5 minutes to soften. Stir the espresso and ⅓ cup of the sugar in a medium saucepan over moderate heat until sugar dissolves. Add gelatin and heat until gelatin dissolves. Chill for 20 minutes, or until mixture becomes syrupy.

2. Using electric mixer at high speed, beat egg white in a small deep bowl until fluffy white. Beat in the remaining sugar, 1 tablespoon at a time, until mixture forms soft peaks. Beat heavy cream in another small deep bowl until stiff.

3. With same beaters, beat slightly chilled gelatin mixture until light and fluffy. Fold in meringue, then stiffly beaten heavy cream, using a whisk, until no streaks of coffee or white remain. Fold in chopped almonds, Marsala wine and lemon rind, just to blend. Spoon into 4 parfait glasses.

4. Chill for 4 hours, or until dessert time. *Serves 4.*

VANILLA ICE CREAM WITH HOT MINCED TOPPING

1 cup prepared mincemeat
½ cup cranberry relish or whole berry
  cranberry sauce

1 fresh pear, pared and cut into chunks
3 tablespoons light rum
1½ pints vanilla ice cream

1. Combine mincemeat and cranberry relish or whole berry cranberry sauce in a heavy skillet; cook over medium heat, stirring often, until heated through. Add pear chunks and mix lightly together; keep warm.

2. Heat rum over medium heat in a small saucepan; *do not boil.*

3. Mound vanilla ice cream in 4 dessert bowls. Remove fruit mixture and rum from heat. Carefully ignite rum, using a long match, and pour over fruit mixture; as flames subside, spoon topping over ice cream. Serve immediately. *Serves 4.*

STRAWBERRY ICE CREAM MERINGUE SUNDAE

3 egg whites
¼ teaspoon cream of tartar
1 cup sugar
1 teaspoon vanilla extract

1 pint strawberries, rinsed and hulled
1 quart strawberry ice cream
stiffly beaten heavy cream or refrigerator
  dessert topping

1. Start this dessert the day before you plan to serve it. Preheat oven to 450° F. Using electric mixer, beat egg whites in small bowl until foamy. Add cream of tartar and continue to beat until soft peaks form.

2. Gradually add sugar and vanilla extract, beating continuously. Continue beating until stiff peaks form.

3. Line two baking sheets with brown paper. Spoon 6 mounds of meringue onto paper, evenly spaced. Use a spoon to shape into 4-inch rounds; slightly hollow out the center of each meringue.

4. Put baking sheets into preheated oven and immediately turn off heat. Leave overnight; do not open door. The following day, take meringue shells out of the oven. Use a spatula to remove shells from paper. Carefully store in a dry place until ready to use.

5. To assemble dessert, first crush the strawberries. Place meringue shells on 6 dessert plates and fill each shell with a generous scoop of strawberry ice cream. Top ice cream with crushed strawberries and whipped cream or whipped topping. *Serves 6.*

STRAWBERRY-PINEAPPLE LITTLE LAYER CAKE

one 9-ounce frozen pound cake, thawed
one 10-ounce package frozen sliced
  strawberries, thawed
one 16-ounce can pineapple chunks

2 tablespoons cornstarch
¼ cup cold water
2 cups heavy cream, stiffly beaten

1. Cut pound cake into 3 horizontal layers. Drain juice from strawberries and pineapple into a 1-cup measure. (If necessary, add water to make 1 cup liquid.) Heat in medium saucepan over low heat.

2. Blend cornstarch in ¼ cup cold water; stir into juices in saucepan. Bring to boiling point, stirring constantly. When juice thickens and becomes transparent, quickly stir in strawberries and pineapple. Remove from heat and cool.

3. When fruit is at room temperature, fold in stiffly beaten heavy cream. Place bottom cake layer on serving plate and spread with about ⅓ of the fruit mixture. Top with second cake layer and ⅓ of the fruit. Top with third layer and the remaining fruit.

4. Chill cake for 30 to 40 minutes before slicing with serrated knife. *Serves 4 to 6.*

CHEESE 'N' SPICE ROLL-UPS

½ cup butter or margarine
one 8-ounce package cream cheese,
  softened
¾ cup sugar
1 egg yolk

2 tablespoons light cream
½ teaspoon vanilla extract
16 slices white bread
¼ cup finely chopped walnuts
1 teaspoon cinnamon

1. Preheat oven to 400° F. Melt butter or margarine in a pie plate in oven.

2. In a small bowl, combine cream cheese, ¼ cup of the sugar, the egg yolk, light cream and vanilla extract until very smooth. On a wooden board, cut crusts from bread with a sharp knife. Using a rolling pin, roll each slice until very thin.

3. Spread cheese mixture on bread slices, dividing evenly. Roll up bread slices. Combine the remaining ½ cup sugar, the chopped walnuts and cinnamon on waxed paper. Dip rolls first into melted butter or margarine, then into the sugar mixture to coat evenly. Arrange roll-ups on a large cookie sheet.

4. Bake for 15 minutes, or until golden. Serve warm. *Serves 8.*

CHILLED CHEESECAKE

about 10 vanilla wafers
2 tablespoons butter or margarine
1 cup sugar
2 envelopes unflavored gelatin
½ teaspoon salt
1 cup milk
2 eggs, separated
3 tablespoons lemon juice

2 teaspoons grated lemon rind
three 8-ounce containers creamed
  cottage cheese
1 cup heavy cream
½ cup sour cream
1 teaspoon sugar
½ teaspoon vanilla extract

1. In electric blender, crush enough vanilla wafers to measure ½ cup. Melt butter or margarine in small saucepan over low heat; lightly brush sides of 9-inch springform pan with some of the melted butter or margarine; sprinkle lightly with some of the vanilla wafer crumbs. Add remaining vanilla wafer crumbs to remaining melted butter or margarine; mix together until well blended and press in bottom of pan; chill while preparing filling.

2. In top of double boiler, combine 1 cup sugar, the gelatin and salt. In small bowl, beat together milk and egg yolks until light and frothy; add to gelatin mixture and place over boiling water. Cook, stirring constantly, for 10 minutes, or until gelatin dissolves and mixture coats back of a metal spoon. Remove from heat and stir in lemon juice and rind; cool.

3. Press cottage cheese through sieve into a medium bowl. Stir in cooled gelatin mixture. Chill, stirring occasionally, until mixture is consistency of unbeaten egg whites.

4. Using electric mixer at high speed, beat egg whites in small bowl until stiff peaks form. In another small bowl, beat heavy cream until stiff. Fold stiffly beaten egg whites, then stiffly beaten heavy cream, into cheese mixture; pour into chilled crumb crust.

5. Combine sour cream, 1 teaspoon sugar and the vanilla extract in a small bowl; spread over top of cheesecake. Chill for 4 to 5 hours, or overnight. *Serves 6 to 8.*

EnergySaving Tip: For a totally no-bake but delicious cheesecake variation, try the following Peach-Chestnut Cheesecake: In a small bowl, blend 1½ cups graham cracker crumbs, ¼ cup brown sugar, firmly packed, and ¼ teaspoon cinnamon; toss with ⅓ cup butter or margarine, melted. Press to line bottom of one 9-inch springform pan, and to line the sides to a depth of 1½ inches. Or use crumb mixture to line a 9-inch pie plate; chill while making filling.

To make filling: In blender container, sprinkle 2 envelopes unflavored gelatin over ¼ cup peach juice from one 20-ounce can peach halves; let soften 5 minutes. Add ½ cup boiling water and ½ cup sugar; process until dissolved and smooth. Place mixture in large bowl; set aside. Place remaining peach juice and peach halves in blender container and process until peaches are chopped; do not process until they are a smooth puree. Add to gelatin mixture in bowl. With electric mixer at high speed, beat in one 16-ounce can chestnut puree, chilled, one 16-ounce container small curd cottage cheese, ¼ cup cream sherry and ½ teaspoon almond extract. In a small bowl, beat 1 cup heavy cream until stiff; fold into peach-chestnut mixture.

Spoon filling into chilled crust; chill cheesecake 4 to 6 hours or overnight. If desired, top cheesecake just before serving with ½ cup sour cream, sprinkled with ¼ cup darkly toasted, slivered almonds.

SICILIAN CHEESECAKE

one 16-ounce container ricotta or
 creamed cottage cheese
¼ cup sugar
1 tablespoon heavy cream
1 tablespoon finely chopped candied
 orange peel or citron

1 tablespoon chopped semisweet
 chocolate
½ teaspoon vanilla extract
one 9-ounce frozen pound cake, thawed
¼ cup Marsala or sherry
Chocolate Frosting (below)

1. Start this dessert the day before you plan to serve it. In medium bowl, thoroughly mix ricotta or cottage cheese, sugar, heavy cream, candied orange peel or citron, semisweet chocolate and vanilla extract. Let stand at room temperature to blend flavors for 30 minutes.

2. Cut pound cake into 4 horizontal slices with a sharp knife. Sprinkle each slice with Marsala or sherry.

3. Place bottom slice on large dessert platter; spread with layer of cheese filling. Repeat with remaining cake slices and filling. (Leave the top slice of cake plain.) Chill filled cake for several hours or until very firm.

4. Meanwhile, make Chocolate Frosting; chill. Spread top and sides of chilled cake with frosting. Cover with waxed paper or plastic wrap; chill overnight. *Serves 4 to 6 generously.*

Chocolate Frosting

8 ounces semisweet chocolate
½ cup strong coffee

½ cup butter or margarine

1. Combine semisweet chocolate and coffee in medium saucepan over low heat. Mix until smooth, stirring constantly.

2. Remove from heat and cool for about 5 minutes. Beat in butter or margarine, 1 tablespoon at a time. Chill until thick enough to spread, about 45 to 60 minutes.

PINEAPPLE CHEESECAKE DESSERT

butter or margarine
1½ cups graham cracker crumbs or
   vanilla wafer crumbs
one 20-ounce can crushed pineapple
1 package unflavored gelatin
one 8-ounce package cream cheese

1 cup sugar
1 teaspoon vanilla extract
one 13-ounce can evaporated milk, well
   chilled
½ cup sour cream
1 tablespoon sugar

1. Butter bottom and sides of 9-inch springform pan. Sprinkle with crumbs to completely cover inside surface of pan.

2. Drain pineapple juice into a 1-cup measure. (If necessary, add water to make 1 cup liquid.) Set crushed pineapple aside for later use.

3. Heat ¾ cup of the pineapple juice in small saucepan. Soften gelatin in remaining ¼ cup juice; dissolve in hot pineapple juice. Cool.

4. Using electric mixer, cream together cream cheese, the 1 cup sugar and the vanilla extract in large bowl until light and fluffy. Stir in cooled gelatin mixture.

5. Using electric mixer at high speed, beat chilled evaporated milk in a chilled bowl with chilled beaters until soft peaks form. Fold into cheese mixture. Pour mixture into prepared springform pan. Chill about 10 minutes until top is firm to touch.

6. In a small bowl, mix sour cream, the 1 tablespoon sugar and the reserved crushed pineapple; spread pineapple topping over cheesecake. Chill at least 3 hours before serving. *Serves 6 generously.*

Note: Two prepared graham cracker pie shells can be used; double the topping mixture of sour cream, sugar and crushed pineapple if two shells are filled.

RICE

TYPES

REGULAR RICE: Outer hull and bran of rice grains are removed by polishing. Long-grain rice is used in curries, Chinese dishes and as a side dish; it cooks fluffy, dry and flaky. Short-grained rice is less expensive, and is used in casseroles, desserts and puddings. Allow 25 minutes to cook. One cup uncooked equals 3 cups cooked rice.

PARBOILED (OR CONVERTED) RICE: Because of its special processing, it contains more vitamins than regular rice. Cooking time is longer; allow 30 to 35 minutes. One cup uncooked equals 3½ cups cooked rice.

QUICK-COOKING (OR INSTANT) RICE: Rice which has been commercially cooked and dried; does not have the traditional texture of regular rice. Can be prepared in 1 to 5 minutes. One cup non-prepared rice equals 2 cups hot rice.

BROWN RICE: A whole-grain rice with only the outer hull removed. Rich in vitamins, it has a nutty flavor and is best used as a side dish or pilaf. Takes longer to cook than regular or parboiled rice; allow 35 to 45 minutes. One cup uncooked equals 4 cups cooked rice.

RICE MIXES: Multi-flavored rice mixes and mixes of varying rice grains (regular and brown, regular and wild, etc.); Carefully follow package directions. One cup uncooked equals about 1½ cups cooked rice.

PAELLA: Spanish chicken and seafood dish containing saffron-flavored rice and vegetables. Rice should be added to the casserole dish 25 minutes before serving.

RISOTTO: Italian-style rice; rice is first lightly sautéed in butter or oil, then simmered in beef or chicken broth. Fresh vegetables, thinly cut, can be added during last 5 minutes of cooking time.

WILD RICE: Not actually a rice grain, but a grass seed most often found in the Great Lakes region of the United States. Very expensive; often combined with brown or regular rice to reduce cost. Allow 40 to 50 minutes to cook. One cup uncooked equals 3 cups cooked rice.

GO-WITHS

BROTHS AND JUICES: Cook rice in chicken or beef broth or bouillon; or use half vegetable juice and half water, or half fruit juice and half water (apple, apricot and orange juice all give excellent flavor).

FATS: Sauté rice slightly before cooking to give flavor, using butter or margarine, bacon fat, or olive or vegetable oil. In addition, an extra tablespoon of one of these can be tossed into hot rice just before serving.

FRUITS: Turn cooked rice into a fruited pilaf. Add dried (or slightly cooked and dried) fruit; raisins, dates, chunks of dried cooked apple or apricot are best. If preferred, toss in drained canned fruit; try apricots, peach slices, grapes, or even fruit cocktail. All make an excellent pilaf to serve with curry.

HERBS: Along with melted butter, toss in chopped fresh parsley, basil, dill or mint. Use dried herbs with caution; toss in just a little dried sage, oregano or thyme, then taste before adding more.

MEATS: Cooked crumbled bacon is ideal, as are slivers of cooked ham, beef or tongue. A dash of seasoning appropriate to the meat is always good (sage for ham and pork, thyme for beef, and grated orange or lemon rind for tongue).

NUTS: Salty, crunchy nuts are perfect tossed into rice; try toasted almonds or walnuts, salty peanuts or cashews, sweet flaked coconut or pistachios.

SPICES: For curry and Chinese dishes, spice-seasoned rice is excellent. A grating of star anise, cinnamon or nutmeg, or a little chopped crystallized ginger will complement most Oriental food.

VEGETABLES: Slivers of asparagus, mushrooms, peas or carrots, cooked in chicken broth and added to rice, also cooked in broth, make risotto. Toss with sliced olives for the best accompaniment to lamb or veal dishes.

GREAT FOR THE GRILL

Although barbecuing has always appealed to cooks, men and women alike, only recently has it been thought of as an energy-saving method of preparing meals. But, consider that charcoal is not very expensive and it can even be reused when it has not been completely burned up. And, of course, cooking outside automatically eliminates kitchen heat and the need to cool the house.

To grill successfully, you should learn a few simple skills. Most important is to preheat the coals correctly. (Take extreme care when lighting them, especially if you are using charcoal starter fluid.)

How long you preheat will depend on the description of the coals in the particular recipe. The following are some rough time estimates to remember.

- Preheat about 20 to 30 minutes for medium coals (mottled, black-white surface and glowing red inside).
- Preheat about 45 minutes for hot coals (totally white surface and glowing white-yellow inside).
- Preheat about 45 to 60 minutes for ashy coals (gray-white in color and beginning to lose their shape).

Always preheat the coals without the metal grill in place; about 5 or 10 minutes before you start to cook, set the grill in place to heat it. When not specified in the recipe, the grill should be set 3 to 4 inches from the coals for thin meats, fish, vegetables and fruit, and about 6 inches from the coals for thick cuts of meat. Where recommended, lightly oil the grill before setting it in place.

Follow each recipe precisely, with these general rules in mind: Marinating meat tenderizes and flavors it; searing meat on both sides over hot coals seals in the juices; brushing with barbecue sauce flavors meat and protects it from drying out (but do not add it too soon or it will burn); wrapping food in foil retains moisture while protecting it from too much heat.

The hottest area in the center of the grill is best for barbecuing meat (a tasty Grilled Steak au Poivre, perhaps, or Lamb Steaks with Mint Sauce). Reserve the cooler area around the perimeter of the grill for vegetables, foil-wrapped Herb Bread or a dessert such as Bananas in Rum.

You might also try Charcoal-Broiled Shrimp and Scallop Skewers, Buttery Barbecued Chicken Breasts, Corned Beef Hash Cocktail Balls, Barbecued Eggplant or Baked Apples on the Grill. Better yet, try several of them for a complete energy-saving meal. Nothing beats food from the grill for saving energy—and for fabulous charcoal-broiled flavor.

CORNED BEEF HASH COCKTAIL BALLS

two 16-ounce cans corned beef hash
1 egg, beaten
½ cup dry seasoned bread crumbs

½ cup butter or margarine, melted
1 cup finely chopped parsley

1. In a large bowl, break up hash. Thoroughly mix with beaten egg and bread crumbs. Shape into 16 to 20 balls the size of an apricot.

2. Place hash balls on a well-oiled grill over medium coals. Brush with melted butter or margarine.

3. Grill hash balls about 4 to 5 minutes, brushing with butter or margarine. Turn frequently.

4. Place the finely chopped parsley in a shallow pan. Roll the cooked hash balls in parsley to coat. Serve with toothpicks. *Serves 4.*

Note: If the mesh of your grill is too wide and the hash balls might fall through, place a wire cake rack over grill and cook balls a few at a time.

SAUSAGES ON THE GRILL

1. Cut ½ pound bratwurst, knockwurst, kielbasa or frankfurters into bite-size pieces; thread on skewers. Grill over hot coals for about 10 minutes, until sausage pieces are well browned and cooked through.

2. Remove sausages from skewers and serve on toothpicks with a choice of dips (below). *Serves about 4.*

Tangy Dip

¼ cup oil
1 tablespoon finely chopped onion
1 tablespoon curry powder

¼ teaspoon garlic salt
½ cup tomato sauce

1. Heat oil in small saucepan. Add onion and sauté with curry powder and garlic salt.

2. Add tomato sauce and bring to boiling point, stirring occasionally. Serve with grilled sausages. *Makes about ¾ cup.*

Creamy Mustard Sauce

1 cup sour cream

1 tablespoon dry mustard or to taste

1. Thoroughly blend sour cream and dry mustard to make a smooth sauce. Cover with plastic wrap and chill until ready to use.

2. Serve with grilled sausages. *Makes about 1 cup.*

CHEESE AND BACON

½ pound Cheddar or Swiss cheese   **bacon slices**

1. Cut Cheddar or Swiss cheese (or other firm cheese) into 1-inch cubes. Wrap in bacon and thread onto skewers. Cook over medium coals for 5 to 7 minutes, or until the cheese is golden and puffy (but still firm enough to slide off the skewers).

2. Serve at once on toothpicks. *Serves about 4.*

TIPSY CHUCK BARBECUE

½ cup soy sauce   **1 teaspoon Worcestershire sauce**
¼ cup water   **¼ teaspoon ginger**
¼ cup Scotch whisky   **1 clove garlic, crushed**
2 tablespoons brown sugar   **2- to 2½-pound chuck steak**

1. In a 2-cup measure, mix soy sauce, water, Scotch whisky, brown sugar, Worcestershire sauce, ginger and garlic. Shake well and let stand a few minutes to blend flavors.

2. Place steak in a glass 13 x 9 x 2-inch baking pan; pierce several times on both sides with a sharp kitchen fork. Pour marinade over steak. Chill for 2 to 3 hours, turning several times.

3. When ready to cook, drain steak and grill over medium coals, 10 to 15 minutes per side. *Serves 4.*

ORIENTAL FLANK STEAK

2-pound flank steak   **1 clove garlic, finely chopped**
¼ cup soy sauce

1. Spread steak flat and use a sharp knife to score both sides in a diamond pattern. Place on a plate and sprinkle both sides with soy sauce and garlic.

2. Chill for 2 to 3 hours, turning the meat once.

3. Grill over medium coals, 4 to 6 minutes per side. Slice on the diagonal to serve. *Serves 4.*

STUFFED FLANK STEAK ON A SPIT

Garlic Basting Sauce (below)
2-pound flank steak
½ teaspoon instant meat tenderizer
2 tablespoons Dijon-style mustard
1½ cups dry bread crumbs

½ cup chopped onion
⅓ cup chopped celery
¼ cup butter or margarine, melted
1 teaspoon poultry seasoning

1. Prepare Garlic Basting Sauce.

2. Spread steak flat and use a sharp knife to lightly score both sides in a diamond pattern. Sprinkle with meat tenderizer according to label directions. Spread one side of the steak with mustard.

3. In a medium bowl, thoroughly mix bread crumbs, onion, celery, melted butter or margarine, and poultry seasoning. Spread stuffing over mustard.

4. Roll steak up jelly-roll fashion; tie with soft string at 2-inch intervals.

5. Balance and secure on spit. Cook over medium coals for 30 to 40 minutes, basting frequently with garlic sauce. *Serves 4.*

Garlic Basting Sauce

½ cup oil
¼ cup vinegar
1 clove garlic, crushed

½ teaspoon dry mustard
salt and pepper to taste

1. In screwtop jar, combine oil, vinegar, garlic, dry mustard and salt and pepper. Shake well.

2. Let stand an hour or more to blend flavors. Shake again before using. *Makes about ¾ cup.*

STEAK IN WINE MARINADE

⅔ cup red wine
¼ cup brandy
2 tablespoons lemon juice
¼ cup chopped onion

¼ teaspoon ginger
¼ teaspoon coriander
¼ teaspoon pepper
2½- to 3-pound sirloin steak

1. In a 13 x 9 x 2-inch baking dish, combine red wine, brandy, lemon juice, onion, ginger, coriander and pepper; mix well. Add steak and turn several times to cover both sides with the marinade.

2. Let stand at room temperature for 4 hours, or refrigerate overnight. Turn meat often while marinating.

3. When ready to cook, drain steak and blot dry on paper towels (reserve the marinade). Grill steak 3 inches from ashy coals, 10 to 14 minutes per side. Remove to a warm platter.

4. Meanwhile, strain marinade into a small saucepan. Simmer rapidly until reduced by half. Pour over steak and serve at once. *Serves 4 to 6.*

GRILLED STEAK AU POIVRE

2½- to 3-pound sirloin steak, 2 inches thick

3 tablespoons cracked peppercorns
1 teaspoon salt

1. Pat steak dry on both sides with paper towels. Place steak on board and press pepper into both sides, using the heel of the hand or smooth side of wooden mallet. Let stand 1 hour at room temperature.

2. Grill steak about 6 inches from hot coals, 10 to 14 minutes per side.

3. Sprinkle with a little salt and serve at once. *Serves 4 to 6.*

SPIT-BARBECUED RUMP ROAST

2 cups vinegar
2 cups water
1 onion, sliced
10 cloves

5 peppercorns
2 bay leaves
1 tablespoon salt
2½-pound lean beef rump roast

1. In a large saucepan, combine vinegar, water, onion, cloves, peppercorns, bay leaves and salt. Bring to a simmer over low heat. Remove from heat and cool.

2. Place beef roast in a large glass or ceramic bowl. Pour the cooled marinade over beef. (The roast should be covered with liquid.)

3. Marinate beef for 2 days in the refrigerator, turning several times each day.

4. When ready to cook, remove beef and pat dry with paper towels; strain and reserve marinade. Balance and secure roast on spit; roast over medium coals for about 1½ hours or until meat thermometer registers 140° to 160° F.

5. During the last 45 minutes of cooking, baste the meat often with marinade. *Serves 4 to 6.*

BARBECUED BEEF SHORT RIBS

4 pounds beef short ribs, well trimmed
½ cup ketchup
¼ cup molasses
¼ cup lemon juice

1 teaspoon dry mustard
¼ teaspoon chili powder
¼ teaspoon garlic salt
¼ teaspoon onion salt

1. Place short ribs in large kettle and add water to cover. Cover and simmer over moderate heat for about 2 hours, or until fork tender.

2. Drain the ribs and pat dry on paper towels.

3. In a 2-cup measure, combine ketchup, molasses, lemon juice, dry mustard, chili powder, garlic salt and onion salt; mix well.

4. Barbecue the ribs over ashy coals for about 15 minutes, turning once and basting on all sides with sauce. *Serves 4.*

TEXAS-STYLE BEEF RIBS

4 pounds beef short ribs
½ cup flour
1 tablespoon salt
¾ teaspoon pepper
¾ teaspoon chili powder
¾ teaspoon crumbled thyme
½ cup vegetable oil

BARBECUE SAUCE
2 cups chopped onion
1 cup dry sherry
½ cup brown sugar, firmly packed
one 3-ounce can tomato paste

1. Wipe short ribs with damp paper towels. In large paper or plastic bag, combine flour, salt, pepper, chili powder and thyme. Add ribs to bag, a few at a time. Shake to coat ribs well.

2. Heat oil in large roasting pan in 350° F oven. Add ribs, turning to coat all sides in oil. Roast 45 to 60 minutes or until just tender, turning and basting frequently with oil in pan.

3. Meanwhile, make barbecue sauce: Combine onions, sherry, brown sugar and tomato paste in medium saucepan. Cover and cook over low heat, stirring frequently, for about 20 minutes until onions are tender.

4. Remove ribs from pan and drain; place on grill, 6 inches from hot coals. Brush thickly with barbecue sauce. Barbecue for 15 to 25 minutes, turning and basting frequently, until beef is very tender. *Serves 4.*

THE BETTER BURGER

2 tablespoons butter or margarine
½ cup celery
2 pounds lean ground beef
2 eggs, beaten

2 teaspoons salt
¼ teaspoon pepper
1 tablespoon Worcestershire sauce

1. Melt butter or margarine in small skillet; add celery and sauté over medium heat for 4 minutes, or until tender and golden.

2. In large bowl, combine sautéed celery, ground beef, beaten eggs, salt, pepper and Worcestershire sauce. Mix lightly but well. Shape into 4 large patties.

3. Grill over hot coals, 5 to 10 minutes per side. *Serves 4.*

LAMB STEAKS WITH MINT SAUCE

5- to 5½-pound leg of lamb
¼ cup butter or margarine
¼ cup vegetable oil

4 cloves garlic, crushed
Mint Sauce (below)
mint sprigs

1. Have the butcher cut the leg of lamb into crosswise slices or steaks, about ½ to ¾ inch thick. Place the steaks on grill, about 4 inches above medium-hot coals.

2. In a small saucepan, heat butter or margarine, oil and garlic. Simmer gently for a minute or two. Brush lamb steaks generously with mixture.

3. Grill steaks about 8 minutes, turn and brush again. Grill about 8 minutes longer, until nicely browned outside, but still pink inside. Serve with Mint Sauce; garnish with sprigs of mint. *Serves 6.*

Mint Sauce

1 cup vinegar
½ cup finely chopped mint leaves

¼ cup sugar

1. In a small saucepan, combine vinegar, mint and sugar. Bring to boiling point.

2. Serve hot, or pour into a covered container and store in refrigerator until needed. *Makes about 1³/₄ cups.*

Note: If you prefer a shortcut or have no fresh mint, there are a number of commercial mint sauces available in the gourmet section of your supermarket. Whatever sauce you choose, warm it before serving.

GRILLED BUTTERFLIED LEG OF LAMB

4- to 5-pound leg of lamb, butterflied
**   (bone removed and meat flattened)**
½ cup Dijon-style mustard
⅓ cup olive oil
⅓ cup soy sauce

2 tablespoons lemon juice
1 teaspoon rosemary
1 teaspoon thyme
1 teaspoon ginger
1 clove garlic, crushed

1. Remove excess fat from butterflied leg of lamb. Spread lamb flat in a large oblong glass or ceramic baking dish.

2. In a 2-cup measure, combine mustard, oil, soy sauce, lemon juice, rosemary, thyme, ginger and garlic. Pour over lamb, turning to coat on both sides. Cover and refrigerate overnight, turning meat several times.

3. Drain lamb, reserving marinade. Grill about 7 inches from hot coals for 20 minutes. Turn and grill for 20 minutes longer. Brush with reserved marinade every 5 minutes while grilling. *Serves 4 to 6.*

Note: If desired, the lamb can be placed on a greased rack in a broiling pan and broiled in preheated oven for 10 minutes per side. Cooking can then be completed over hot coals.

LAMB AND FRUIT SKEWERS

1 cup soy sauce
½ cup pineapple juice
¼ cup sherry
¼ cup brown sugar, firmly packed
1 teaspoon salt
1 clove garlic, crushed
2 pounds boneless lamb, cut into 1½-inch cubes

1 cantaloupe, pared and cut into large chunks
2 bananas, peeled and cut into 1-inch pieces
one 12-ounce jar preserved kumquats
one 8-ounce can pineapple chunks, drained

1. In small bowl, combine soy sauce, pineapple juice, sherry, brown sugar, salt and garlic; mix well.

2. Pour over lamb cubes in shallow bowl. Cover and refrigerate several hours or overnight.

3. When ready to cook, drain lamb cubes, reserving marinade. Thread lamb on skewers, alternating with cantaloupe, banana, kumquats and pineapple.

4. Brush skewers with marinade and grill about 6 inches above hot coals. Turn and baste until done, about 15 to 20 minutes. *Serves 4. (Shown on page 52.)*

LAMB SHASHLIK

2 pounds lean boneless lamb, cut into 1½-inch cubes
1 cup chopped onion
1 clove garlic, crushed
¾ cup red wine
¾ cup wine vinegar
¼ cup water
¼ teaspoon ground cloves

¼ teaspoon ground cinnamon
5 peppercorns
8 mushroom caps
8 cherry tomatoes
8 small potatoes, precooked
8 pieces green pepper (1-inch squares)
olive oil

1. In a medium bowl, toss lamb cubes with onion and garlic.

2. In a medium saucepan, combine wine, vinegar, water, cloves, cinnamon and peppercorns; bring to boiling point. Cool for a few minutes before pouring over lamb cubes.

3. Allow lamb to marinate at room temperature for several hours, or overnight in refrigerator.

4. When ready to cook, drain lamb and pat dry between paper towels. Thread lamb on skewers, alternating with mushrooms, tomatoes, potatoes and green pepper squares.

5. Brush skewers with olive oil and arrange on grill 4 to 5 inches above hot coals. Grill about 15 to 20 minutes, turning skewers often to brown evenly. *Serves 4.*

Note: Small canned potatoes can be used if desired. Rinse well under cold running water and pat dry before using.

LAMB IN PITA BREAD

⅔ cup red wine
¼ cup oil
¼ cup lemon juice
¼ teaspoon oregano
¼ teaspoon basil
1 bay leaf
1 clove garlic, crushed
salt and pepper to taste

2 pounds lean lamb cubes
¼ cup green pepper squares
¼ cup onion chunks
½ cup button mushrooms
½ cup halved cherry tomatoes
one 8-ounce can tomato sauce
1 package pita bread (4 pockets)

1. In a 2-cup measure, combine wine, oil, lemon juice, oregano, basil, bay leaf, garlic, salt and pepper. Pour over lamb cubes in shallow bowl.

2. Cover and refrigerate for 24 hours, turning lamb often. About 30 minutes before cooking, add green pepper, onion, mushrooms and cherry tomatoes to the bowl.

3. When ready to cook, drain lamb cubes and vegetables; thread on skewers. Grill over hot coals for 15 to 20 minutes, turning frequently.

4. Place tomato sauce in small saucepan and heat on edge of grill. Make slit along one edge of each pita bread to form an open pocket; wrap in aluminum foil and keep hot on the edge of the grill.

5. When skewers are done, push off lamb and vegetables into open pockets of pita bread. Spoon a little hot tomato sauce into and over the pockets. *Serves 4.*

BARBECUED PORK CHOPS

⅓ cup ketchup
¼ cup vinegar
¼ cup water
2 tablespoons oil

1 teaspoon dry mustard
1 teaspoon salt
1 teaspoon sugar
4 lean loin pork chops, 1 inch thick

1. In a small saucepan, mix ketchup, vinegar, water, oil, dry mustard, salt and sugar. Bring to boiling point. Reduce heat to medium and simmer for 5 minutes.

2. Place pork chops on the grill over ashy coals. After 5 minutes, begin basting with ketchup mixture and turning chops.

3. Continue to baste and turn chops until they are browned and tender and cooked through to the center, about 45 minutes. *Serves 4.*

PORK SATES

2 pounds lean boneless pork
1 cup orange juice
3 tablespoons lemon juice
2 tablespoons soy sauce

2 cloves garlic, crushed
1 tablespoon brown sugar
¼ cup oil
Peanut Sauce (below)

1. Trim all fat from pork. Cut the meat into 1½-inch cubes. Place cubes in shallow glass 13 x 9 x 2-inch baking dish.

2. In a 2-cup measure, mix orange juice, lemon juice, soy sauce, garlic and brown sugar. Pour over pork cubes. Refrigerate overnight, stirring several times.

3. When ready to cook, dry pork on paper towels and thread on skewers. Place on grill about 10 inches above hot coals.

4. Brush pork with oil and turn often. Pork should be well done in about 20 minutes, but may take a little longer if coals are not hot enough.

5. Meanwhile, prepare Peanut Sauce. When pork is cooked through, serve at once with sauce. *Serves 4.*

Peanut Sauce

1 teaspoon butter or margarine
1 tablespoon soy sauce
4 tablespoons peanut butter

1 tablespoon lemon juice
⅛ teaspoon cayenne or to taste
½ cup heavy cream

1. In a small saucepan, mix butter or margarine, soy sauce, peanut butter, lemon juice and cayenne. Simmer over low heat for 10 minutes, stirring frequently.

2. Stir in heavy cream and keep hot until ready to serve. If sauce separates slightly, stir in 1 to 2 tablespoons cold water, or an ice cube. *Makes about 1 cup.*

INDIAN PORK CUBES

½ cup chutney
¼ cup ketchup
2 tablespoons soy sauce
2 tablespoons oil

2 pounds boneless pork loin or fresh ham,
cut into 1-inch cubes
½ cup finely chopped peanuts (optional)

1. In electric blender, puree chutney. Add ketchup, soy sauce and oil. Process on mix for a few seconds. Pour mixture over pork cubes in glass bowl. Marinate in refrigerator for several hours, turning pork often.

2. Thread pork on skewers and grill about 30 minutes over medium coals. Turn often to brown on all sides. Pork should be crisply brown and well done.

3. For extra crunch, roll the cooked pork cubes in chopped peanuts. *Serves 4 to 6.*

CHINESE SPARERIBS

5 tablespoons Hoisin sauce
3 tablespoons soy sauce
3 tablespoons sherry

1 clove garlic, crushed
4 pounds meaty pork spareribs
2 cups hot water

1. In a small bowl, mix Hoisin sauce, soy sauce, sherry and garlic. Brush generously over both sides of spareribs; let stand for 2 hours.

2. Preheat oven to 350° F. Pour 2 cups of hot water into a large roasting pan. Spread spareribs on rack in pan. Roast 30 minutes, adding more hot water if needed. Brush ribs with sauce; turn, brush again and cook for 30 minutes longer. (You can cook the ribs to this point early in the day, or even the night before, and then finish cooking it on the grill.)

3. Place spareribs on grill over hot coals; grill for 10 to 15 minutes per side, or until well browned. The ribs will be crisper if you cut the sparerib rack into 3-rib sections before grilling. *Serves 4 to 6.*

FEISTY SPARERIBS

4 pounds spareribs
1½ cups ketchup
½ cup vinegar
2 teaspoons sugar
½ teaspoon salt
pinch of pepper

¼ whole lemon, finely chopped
  (including rind)
1 teaspoon coriander
½ teaspoon cumin
¼ teaspoon ginger
drop hot pepper sauce

1. Spread spareribs on grill over hot coals. Cook and turn until well browned on both sides, about 50 minutes in all.

2. Meanwhile, combine ketchup, vinegar, sugar, salt and pepper in a medium saucepan. Bring to boiling point, reduce heat and simmer for 10 minutes.

3. Stir in lemon, coriander, cumin, ginger and hot pepper sauce. Continue to simmer for 5 minutes longer.

4. When ribs are well browned, baste one side, cook for a few minutes and turn. Repeat until sauce is used and ribs are done, about 10 minutes longer altogether. Be sure the ribs are thoroughly cooked, but watch closely to prevent flare-ups. *Serves 4.*

CRUNCHY PORK LOIN ON A SPIT

5-pound pork loin, boned, rolled and tied
¾ cup apple butter or apple jelly
¼ cup chunky peanut butter

3 tablespoons frozen orange juice
concentrate

1. Balance and secure pork loin on a spit, making sure spit turns smoothly. Roast over medium coals about 3 hours. If using a meat thermometer, temperature should read 170° F.

2. Beat the apple butter or jelly into the peanut butter; beat in the orange juice concentrate. Brush over the roast about 15 minutes before pork is done. Continue to cook until pork is cooked through and has a crisp and crunchy surface. *Serves 8.*

GRILLED HAM STEAKS

½ cup butter or margarine, melted
1 cup sherry
1 cup pineapple juice
1 teaspoon whole cloves

¼ cup dark brown sugar, firmly packed
1 clove garlic, crushed
2 center-cut ham slices, 1 inch thick

1. In a 4-cup measure or medium bowl, combine melted butter or margarine, sherry, pineapple juice, cloves, brown sugar and garlic. Mix well.

2. Place ham steaks in single layer in shallow dish or pan. Pour marinade over ham. Marinate in refrigerator at least 6 hours or overnight. For maximum flavor, allow to stand at room temperature for at least ⅓ of the marinating time.

3. When ready to cook, drain ham steaks and slash edges to prevent curling; reserve marinade. Grill steaks over medium-hot coals for about 10 minutes per side.

4. During last 5 minutes of grilling, brush ham steaks generously with reserved marinade. *Serves 4 to 6.*

HAM AND FRUIT KABOBS

2½ pounds fully cooked boneless ham,
   cut into 1½-inch cubes
one 18-ounce jar spiced crab apples,
   drained
one 16-ounce can pineapple chunks,
   drained

½ cup ketchup
½ cup orange marmalade
2 tablespoons vegetable oil
1 tablespoon vinegar
1 teaspoon dry mustard

1. Alternate ham cubes, crab apples and pineapple chunks on skewers.

2. In a small bowl, mix ketchup, marmalade, oil, vinegar and dry mustard. Set aside.

3. Grill kabobs over medium-hot coals, turning frequently, for about 8 to 10 minutes. During last 5 minutes, brush kabobs generously with marmalade sauce. Serve any extra sauce with grilled kabobs. *Serves 4 to 6.*

SPIT-ROASTED CANADIAN BACON

⅓ cup sherry
½ cup orange marmalade
¼ teaspoon powdered ginger

1½ pounds fully cooked Canadian bacon,
  in one piece

1. In a small saucepan, mix sherry, marmalade and ginger. Bring to boiling point, stirring constantly. Set aside until ready to use.

2. Balance and secure the bacon on a spit over a drip pan. Roast over medium-hot coals for 1 hour and 15 minutes.

3. After 1 hour, brush bacon with the marmalade sauce. Continue to baste often for the final 15 minutes of roasting.

4. Let the glazed and browned roast stand for 5 minutes before slicing. *Serves 4 to 6.*

CHARCOAL-BROILED CHICKEN LIVERS

1 pound chicken livers
¼ pound sliced bacon
2 cups whole mushrooms
12 small white onions, parboiled

1 clove garlic, crushed
3 tablespoons oil
1 teaspoon salt
¼ teaspoon pepper

1. Cut the chicken livers in half, cut bacon slices into squares, and wipe and trim the mushrooms.

2. Thread the chicken livers, bacon, mushrooms and onions on skewers. In a cup, mix garlic, oil, salt and pepper; brush over skewers.

3. Grill over medium coals, turning and basting, for about 15 minutes. Watch closely to prevent overcooking. *Serves 4 to 6.*

BROTHER-IN-LAW CHICKEN

two 2½-pound broiler-fryer chickens, cut
  into serving pieces
¾ cup fresh lime juice

1 teaspoon salt
¼ teaspoon pepper
½ cup butter or margarine, melted

1. Place chicken pieces in a single layer in a large shallow baking dish. Combine ½ cup of the lime juice, salt and pepper; pour over chicken. Marinate in refrigerator for several hours, turning chicken often.

2. In a small saucepan, heat melted butter or margarine with remaining ¼ cup lime juice; keep warm.

3. When ready to cook, place chicken pieces on grill over ashy coals; brush with lime butter. As chicken browns, turn and brush frequently with more lime butter. Grill for 45 to 60 minutes. *Serves 4 to 6.*

CHICKEN CAYMAN

two 2- to 2½-pound frying chickens, quartered
½ cup lime or lemon juice
½ cup oil
1 clove garlic, crushed

1 teaspoon salt
¼ teaspoon chervil
⅛ teaspoon cinnamon
⅛ teaspoon pepper
⅛ teaspoon cardamom

1. Rinse chickens; dry on paper towels. Spread in single layer in large baking dish.

2. In screwtop jar, mix lime or lemon juice, oil, garlic, salt, chervil, cinnamon, pepper and cardamom. Shake well to mix thoroughly; let stand about 10 minutes. Shake well again and pour over chicken pieces. Cover and refrigerate overnight.

3. When ready to cook, drain chicken pieces, reserving marinade. Place chicken skin side down on grill, about 6 inches (or more) from medium coals. Grill chicken for about 1 hour, turning several times and brushing often with reserved marinade. *Serves 4 to 6.*

BUTTERY BARBECUED CHICKEN BREASTS

4 large chicken breasts, halved
1 cup butter or margarine
4 cloves garlic, slivered
2 tablespoons chopped parsley

2 tablespoons Worcestershire sauce
1 teaspoon rosemary
salt and pepper to taste

1. Arrange chicken breasts close together in a 13 x 9 x 2-inch baking dish.

2. In a small skillet, melt butter or margarine; add and brown the slivered garlic. Remove garlic with a slotted spoon. Stir in parsley and simmer for 2 minutes.

3. Stir in Worcestershire sauce, rosemary, salt and pepper. Pour over chicken in baking dish. Cover and store in a cool place for 4 to 5 hours, or refrigerate overnight.

4. Place chicken breasts on grill at least 8 to 10 inches above hot coals to prevent butter from flaming up. Grill, turning often, for about 30 minutes, until browned and fork tender. Meanwhile, heat marinade in small saucepan; brush chicken frequently with marinade while grilling. *Serves 4.*

Grilled Salmon Steaks (page 93)

Pizza Dinner (pages 118 and 119)

Canton Chicken Dinner (pages 122 and 123)

Coeur à la Crème (page 26)

BARBECUED BROILER WITH TARRAGON

4-pound broiling chicken, quartered
salt and pepper to taste
1 cup dry white wine

1 cup vegetable oil
2 to 3 tablespoons dried tarragon

1. Place chicken in a 13 x 9 x 2-inch baking dish. Sprinkle with salt and pepper. Mix wine, oil and dried tarragon; pour over chicken. Cover and refrigerate overnight.

2. When ready to cook, place chicken on double thickness of heavy-duty aluminum foil. Pour some of the marinade over chicken, bring up foil and fold into a secure packet to hold in all the juices.

3. Place packet of chicken directly on a bed of ashy coals. Place some of the coals on top of packet. Cook for 1 hour and 15 minutes. Replace top coals once or twice to keep heat even.

4. At end of cooking time, remove packet from coals. Cut a crisscross opening in top of packet and pull back foil. Remove chicken to 4 serving plates. Spoon juices from packet over chicken. *Serves 4.*

LEMONY CHICKEN

4-pound roasting chicken, cut into
   8 pieces
1 cup lemon juice
¼ cup vegetable oil

¼ cup white wine
1 teaspoon salt
¼ teaspoon pepper
vegetable oil

1. Arrange chicken in shallow glass 13 x 9 x 2-inch baking dish. Mix lemon juice, ¼ cup vegetable oil, wine, salt and pepper. Pour over chicken.

2. Turn chicken pieces in marinade so that all are well coated. Cover and refrigerate overnight, turning chicken several times.

3. When ready to cook, dry chicken on paper towels; reserve marinade. Brush chicken with a little vegetable oil and arrange on grill over hot coals. If desired, sprinkle with additional salt and pepper.

4. Grill chicken for about 45 minutes, until crispy brown and fork tender. Turn and brush with more oil as needed.

5. In a small saucepan, simmer reserved marinade rapidly until reduced by half; serve with chicken. *Serves 4.*

YOGURT CHICKEN

2 cups unflavored yogurt
1 teaspoon ginger
1 teaspoon cinnamon
1 clove garlic, crushed

1 teaspoon salt
drop hot pepper sauce
2½- to 3-pound broiler-fryer chicken, cut into serving pieces

1. In small bowl, combine yogurt, ginger, cinnamon, garlic, salt and hot pepper sauce. Let stand about 30 minutes to blend flavors.

2. Spread chicken in single layer in shallow pan. Pour over marinade, cover and refrigerate overnight.

3. When ready to cook, drain the chicken; reserve marinade. Arrange chicken skin side up on a well-oiled grill over hot coals.

4. Grill chicken slowly for about 45 to 60 minutes, until fork tender and golden, turning and basting often with marinade. *Serves 4.*

ORIENTAL BAKED CHICKEN BREASTS

3 whole chicken breasts, halved
⅓ cup Hoisin sauce
⅓ cup soy sauce

⅓ cup sherry
⅓ cup brown sugar, firmly packed
2 cloves garlic, crushed

1. Trim the chicken breasts into shapely pieces, removing skin if desired. Spread in single layer in 13 x 9 x 2-inch baking dish.

2. In a 2-cup measure, mix Hoisin sauce, soy sauce, sherry, brown sugar and garlic. Pour over chicken; marinate 4 to 6 hours.

3. When ready to cook, drain the chicken; reserve marinade. Using a covered grill, place chicken on rack over a drip pan. Cover and grill chicken over medium coals for 1 hour, basting often with marinade. *Serves 4 to 6.*

Note: The special flavor of this recipe depends on its being cooked in a covered grill. However, it can also be prepared by cooking the chicken in an uncovered grill, 4 inches above medium coals. Grill for 45 minutes, turning frequently and basting with marinade.

GRILLED TURKEY

6- to 8-pound turkey   **butter or margarine, melted**

1. A covered grill is necessary for this recipe. Half an hour before you plan to start the turkey, arrange two piles of coals on either side of the bottom of the grill. Place a drip pan in the middle. Start the coals and let them burn down to a gray ash.

2. Truss the turkey for roasting. (It is better not to stuff the turkey because this greatly increases the cooking time; cook stuffing separately by wrapping it in aluminum foil and placing it next to the bird for the last 45 minutes of cooking.) Insert a meat thermometer in the turkey and place turkey on grill over the drip pan. Brush turkey all over with melted butter or margarine.

3. Close the cover of the grill, making sure the dampers are open. Grill the turkey over ashy coals until meat thermometer reads 185° F, about 2 to 2¾ hours. Baste with more melted butter or margarine every 30 minutes. At the end of each hour, add a large handful of coals to the piles on either side of the grill. *Serves about 8.*

CORNISH GAME HENS, SPIT ROASTED

4 frozen Cornish game hens, thawed   **½ cup butter or margarine**
  (about 1 pound each)   **½ teaspoon thyme**
1 teaspoon salt   **¼ teaspoon crumbled rosemary**

1. Wash hens and pat dry. Rub cavity of each hen with ¼ teaspoon salt. Fasten neck skin to back of bird with a small metal skewer. Tie wings to breast with string and tie legs securely to tail.

2. Arrange and secure hens on spit either lengthwise or crosswise, taking care to balance the weight to avoid straining the rotisserie motor.

3. Melt butter or margarine with thyme and rosemary in a small saucepan. Brush herb butter over hens as they start to cook.

4. Roast over ashy coals for 45 minutes to 1 hour and 15 minutes, basting with herb butter every 10 minutes. Hens are fully cooked when the drumstick can be twisted easily and the juices run clear. *Serves 4.*

GLAZED DUCKLING

4- to 4½-pound duckling, quartered
1 teaspoon salt
½ cup apricot preserves

¼ cup lemon juice
1 tablespoon soy sauce
orange juice

1. Rinse duckling and pat dry on paper towels. Remove as much fat as possible.

2. Sprinkle the duckling with salt and place skin side up on grill, about 8 inches above medium coals. Place a drip pan under the duckling to catch drippings and prevent flare-ups. Grill duckling for about 1 hour, turning several times.

3. In a small saucepan, combine apricot preserves, lemon juice and soy sauce. Stir over low heat. If the mixture is very thick, thin with orange juice to a medium-thick consistency. About 10 minutes before the duckling is done, brush generously on both sides with the apricot sauce. *Serves 4.*

GRILLED BLUEFISH

2 pounds bluefish fillets
½ cup butter or margarine
1 teaspoon salt
¼ teaspoon pepper

LEMON BUTTER SAUCE
⅓ cup butter or margarine
⅓ cup lemon juice
2 tablespoons capers, chopped

1. Grease a hinged grill made especially for outdoor cooking. Place the fillets flat on the grill; dot generously with some of the ½ cup butter or margarine, and sprinkle with salt and pepper. Close grill and secure handle. Melt remaining butter or margarine.

2. Place hinged grill on top of regular grill; cook fish on both sides over hot coals, brushing several times with melted butter or margarine.

3. Grill until fish flakes easily with a fork, about 8 to 10 minutes. Serve at once with a lemon butter sauce made by combining and heating the ⅓ cup butter or margarine, the lemon juice and capers in a small saucepan. *Serves 4.*

EnergySaving Tip: Food that has been improperly cooked means energy has been wasted. Here are a few tips on barbecuing to ensure tasty and energy-efficient results every time.
• Foods with a moderate proportion of fat, particularly hamburger, sausage and duckling, tend to cause flame flare-ups when the fat melts into the hot barbecue coals. Never spray the coals with water to put out the flames. Instead, cover the entire barbecue grill with a sheet of heavy-duty foil. This will cut off the air supply and smother the flames. It is a good idea to have a couple of sheets on hand when you're barbecuing, just for this purpose.
• When foods are cooked and the coals are still glowing but only half used, do not let them burn down and be wasted. The fire can be put out right away and the coals reused later. Put out the fire by spraying *lightly* with water and then covering the entire barbecue grill with heavy-duty foil to cut off the air supply.

STUFFED BLUEFISH

3-pound bluefish
two 6½-ounce cans crabmeat, drained,
  flaked and cartilage removed
1 egg, beaten
¼ cup heavy cream

3 tablespoons sherry
1 tablespoon seasoned bread crumbs
parsley
lemon wedges
butter pats

1. Scale and clean fish, slitting open one side for stuffing. Rinse thoroughly and pat dry on paper towels.

2. In medium bowl, mix crabmeat, beaten egg, heavy cream, sherry and bread crumbs. Stuff bluefish with this mixture. Close opening with small skewers or toothpicks.

3. Wrap fish in two lightly oiled layers of heavy-duty aluminum foil, sealing with a double fold to make a tight package. Place the fish package directly on hot coals and bake for 25 to 30 minutes, turning once or twice. Fish is done when it flakes easily with a fork.

4. Loosen fish from foil and garnish with parsley and lemon wedges. Pass extra butter pats separately. *Serves 4.*

GRILLED SALMON STEAKS

2 pounds salmon steaks, 1 inch thick
1½ teaspoons salt
½ teaspoon pepper
½ cup dry white wine

2 drops hot pepper sauce
fresh dill
1 lemon, thinly sliced

1. Season salmon steaks well with salt and pepper.

2. Grill steaks over medium coals for 5 to 8 minutes per side. Baste often with wine seasoned with hot pepper sauce.

3. Grill until salmon flakes easily with a fork. Garnish with dill and lemon slices. *Serves 4.* *(Shown on page 85.)*

EnergySaving Tip: Broiling, grilling or barbecuing fish outdoors is always tricky. If it's not done skillfully, precious energy and expensive food are easily wasted. For the best results, remember:
• Use a hinged grill made especially for barbecuing fish. The square or oblong grill is best for cooking flat pieces of fish such as fillets or steaks. Place over the regular grill of the barbecue.
• For whole fish or whole stuffed fish, use a hinged grill in a fish shape.
• Brush the meshes of the grill very well with oil before placing the fish inside; this will ensure easy removal once the fish is cooked.
• An alternate method of barbecuing fish is to wrap and cook the fillets, steaks or whole fish in oiled aluminum foil.
• Fish cooks quickly and can easily be overcooked; watch carefully and baste with butter, margarine or oil during the cooking process.
• After cooking, remove the hinged grill or foil carefully so as not to tear the outer skin or flesh of the fish.

GRILLED SOFT-SHELL CRABS

12 fresh or frozen (and thawed) soft-shell
crabs
½ cup butter or margarine

3 tablespoons lemon juice
1 tablespoon chopped parsley
lemon wedges

1. Rinse crabs and pat dry on paper towels. Arrange on well-greased hinged grill made especially for outdoor cooking. Brush crabs with melted butter or margarine, mixed with lemon juice and parsley.

2. Close grill and secure handle; set hinged grill on top of regular grill, about 6 inches above medium coals. Grill crabs about 5 minutes per side (less if very small), brushing often with butter sauce.

3. When crabs are nicely browned, drizzle with remaining butter sauce; serve with lemon wedges. *Serves 4 to 6.*

SCALLOPS AND BACON EN BROCHETTE

½ cup butter or margarine
2 tablespoons lime or lemon juice
2 tablespoons chopped parsley

24 sea scallops, rinsed and dried
fine dry seasoned bread crumbs
8 slices bacon

1. In small saucepan, melt butter or margarine; stir in lime or lemon juice and parsley. Dip scallops in butter mixture, then roll in fine bread crumbs.

2. Thread 6 scallops onto each of 4 skewers, weaving 2 slices bacon between scallops.

3. Grill skewers for 8 to 10 minutes over hot coals, turning often to brown evenly.

4. Reheat remaining butter sauce and pour over scallops; serve at once. *Serves 4.*

CHARCOAL-BROILED SHRIMP AND SCALLOP SKEWERS

1 pound large shrimp, peeled and
deveined (leave last section of shell and
tail intact)
1 pound scallops
¼ cup oil
¼ cup soy sauce

¼ cup lemon juice
1 clove garlic, crushed
½ teaspoon dry mustard
salt and pepper to taste
1 tablespoon chopped parsley
lemon wedges

1. In large non-metallic bowl, mix shrimp, scallops, oil, soy sauce, lemon juice, garlic, dry mustard, salt and pepper. Toss and mix well to thoroughly coat shrimp and scallops with marinade. Let stand at room temperature for 1 hour, or in refrigerator for several hours. Mix several times while marinating. When ready to cook, drain shellfish; reserve marinade.

2. Place skewers on well-oiled grill about 6 inches above medium-hot coals. Turn and brush often with marinade. Broil until shrimp turns pink and scallops are creamy white and opaque, about 8 to 10 minutes.

3. To serve, brush with marinade, sprinkle with parsley and garnish with lemon wedges. *Serves 4.*

BARBECUED LOBSTER TAILS

8 frozen rock lobster tails (about 8 ounces each)
3 tablespoons butter or margarine

3 tablespoons lemon juice
2 tablespoons chopped parsley

1. Thaw lobster tails. Cut away underside membrane; rinse and dry tails. Bend tails until shell cracks to prevent curling on grill (or insert a metal skewer lengthwise through meat so tail will lie flat).

2. Melt butter or margarine with lemon juice and parsley in a small saucepan. Brush lobster meat with butter mixture. Place shell side up on grill, about 6 inches above medium coals.

3. Broil 8 to 10 minutes. Turn, brush lobster meat generously with butter sauce and cook 5 to 7 minutes longer. Lobster tails are done when meat is firm and opaque. *Serves 4.*

GRILLED BAKED POTATOES

4 Idaho baking potatoes
salt

4 tablespoons butter or margarine

1. Scrub and dry potatoes. Wrap potatoes in aluminum foil for a steamed texture; leave unwrapped for a fluffy texture.

2. Place potatoes in bottom of grill, next to (not on) hot coals. Turn frequently for about 1 hour, depending on size of potato. When potatoes squeeze easily and are fork tender, remove from grill. Cut open, sprinkle with salt and place 1 tablespoon butter in each slit. *Serves 4.*

GRILLED SWEET POTATOES

8 small sweet potatoes

butter or margarine

1. In medium saucepan, boil unpeeled, whole sweet potatoes in salted water to cover. Cook about ½ hour until fork tender; drain and cool.

2. Place potatoes on grill over medium coals and cook 20 minutes. Turn several times to avoid burning.

3. When ready to serve, cut open; dot with butter or margarine. *Serves 4.*

ZIPPY POTATOES

4 potatoes   **¼ cup butter or margarine**
half of ¾-ounce envelope onion soup mix

1. Peel potatoes and cut into quarters or large pieces; rinse. With some water still adhering to potato pieces, place them on a large piece of heavy-duty aluminum foil.

2. Sprinkle with onion soup mix and dot with butter or margarine.

3. Wrap the aluminum foil around the potatoes, sealing carefully. Place on grill over medium coals; grill for about 25 minutes. *Serves 4.*

CORN ON THE COB, TWO WAYS

corn on cob   **salt and pepper**
butter or margarine

Method 1

1. Hull and rinse corn. Place each ear on a square of heavy-duty aluminum foil. Brush with butter or margarine and sprinkle with salt and pepper.

2. Wrap the aluminum foil closely around each ear of corn and place on grill over hot coals. Roast about 20 to 25 minutes, turning several times with tongs.

Method 2

1. Peel back but do not pull off corn husks. Remove all silk from ears of corn. Replace the husks by pulling them up around each ear. Use string or thin wire to tie the husks closely around the corn, covering each ear completely.

2. Soak the ears in water for 15 minutes; drain well. Place on grill over hot coals. Allow ears to steam about 20 to 25 minutes, turning several times with tongs.

BARBECUED EGGPLANT

⅓ cup vegetable oil   **¼ teaspoon oregano**
2 tablespoons vinegar   **¼ teaspoon basil**
1 clove garlic, crushed   **1 large eggplant, unpeeled**
1 teaspoon salt

1. In 1-cup measure, mix oil, vinegar, garlic, salt, oregano and basil. Cut eggplant lengthwise into 4 wedges. Stir oil mixture and brush generously all over eggplant.

2. Place eggplant wedges on grill about 4 inches above medium-hot coals. Grill about 10 minutes, turning often and brushing frequently with oil mixture until it is all gone. Eggplant is ready when tender and easily pierced with a fork. *Serves 4.*

HERB BREAD

1 long loaf French bread
½ cup butter or margarine
¼ cup grated Parmesan cheese
1 tablespoon chopped parsley

½ teaspoon garlic salt
¼ teaspoon oregano
¼ teaspoon basil

1. Cut French bread in diagonal slices almost through to bottom crust.

2. In small saucepan, melt butter or margarine. Stir in cheese, parsley, garlic salt, oregano and basil. Mix well and brush on all cut surfaces of bread.

3. Wrap in aluminum foil and place over medium coals on edge of grill to heat through. *Serves 4 to 6.*

BANANAS IN RUM

4 bananas, peeled and halved lengthwise
¼ cup butter or margarine
¼ cup brown sugar, firmly packed

1 teaspoon cinnamon
¼ cup rum (or orange juice)

1. On a large sheet of wide heavy-duty aluminum foil, arrange banana halves in single layer. Dot with butter or margarine and sprinkle with brown sugar and cinnamon.

2. Fold aluminum foil carefully around bananas to make a leakproof packet. Place the packet 3 to 4 inches above medium coals for 12 to 15 minutes. Bananas should be soft but not mushy.

3. When bananas are almost done, carefully cut a crisscross opening in top of packet. Warm rum in a metal measuring cup, pour over bananas and ignite at once; when flames subside, dessert is ready. (Or pour ¼ cup orange juice over bananas before serving.) *Serves 4.*

BAKED APPLES ON THE GRILL

4 large baking apples
¼ cup sugar

¼ cup butter or margarine
1 teaspoon cinnamon

1. Core apples and fill each center with 1 tablespoon sugar, 1 tablespoon butter or margarine, and ¼ teaspoon cinnamon.

2. Wrap each apple in a square of heavy-duty aluminum foil. Cook over hot coals about 8 inches from center of grill for about 30 minutes. *Serves 4.*

SALAD MAKINGS

LETTUCE

BOSTON: Sometimes called butter lettuce because of its soft, buttery leaves, which deepen to pale green. A not-so-crisp lettuce, its small head serves only 2 to 3 people. It has a mild flavor and is best used as part of a simple green salad, or as a garnish for a strongly seasoned salad.

BIBB: A very small version of Boston lettuce; allow one tiny head per person. Sometimes called limestone lettuce because of its flavor, or lamb's tongue lettuce because of its red-tipped leaves. Its mild flavor is a perfect foil for expensive salad ingredients.

CURLY CHICORY: An inexpensive, strong-flavored salad green, easily recognizable by its massive curly head with leaves ranging in color from deep green to pale yellow. Wash well before using; toss with strong-flavored salad ingredients, or use the fronds to garnish meat and poultry dishes.

ENDIVE: Imported from Belgium, these pale, white-gold, spearlike leaves cluster around one another to form small bundles. Tear into bite-size pieces (don't cut), and prepare only at last moment. A distinctive, slightly bitter flavor; perfect with watercress sprigs, and dressed with vinaigrette.

ESCAROLE: A robust, bushy lettuce with spearlike leaves which have scalloped edges; it has a distinct bitter flavor. Perfect as a base for hearty salads tossed with heavy dressings. A lettuce which remains crisp when part of a salad.

ICEBERG: The most popular lettuce; remains crisp a long time if not broken into separate leaves before storing. Sturdy and robust, this lettuce has no unique flavor and thus can be used in any style salad, and also with strong-flavored dressings.

ROMAINE: A robust, long-leaved, pale-to-deep-green lettuce, almost like a hearty, deep-flavored Chinese cabbage. Another lettuce suited for making hearty salads and tossing with heavier-than-usual dressings. Its classic use is in Caesar salad.

SPINACH: One of many leafy green vegetables that are good alternatives to lettuce; deep flavored and robust in texture, it can be used in hot or cold salads. Shredded cabbage, celery fronds and watercress sprigs are also good green vegetables for salads.

VEGETABLES

ASPARAGUS: In season, the finger-thin stems of young shoots can be thinly sliced and tossed into salads; toss the fresh asparagus tips in whole. Or simmer the whole spear slightly before tossing with oil and vinegar or mayonnaise. Out of season, use canned or frozen asparagus.

BROCCOLI: Unusual and pungent, tiny broccoli florets add variety and flavor to salads, as do tiny cauliflower florets. Raw vegetable salads can be made ahead of time, tossed with dressing and refrigerated; they do not wilt, and only gain in flavor.

BEANS: Young, fresh green beans and wax beans, cut into 1-inch pieces, are ideal salad additions. Out of season, consider frozen lima beans, cooked. Hearty canned chili beans, or kidney, pinto or navy beans in a garlicky dressing are also quick salad makings.

MUSHROOMS: Wiped clean and sliced very thinly, these are best served by themselves in a delicate parsley vinaigrette dressing. Or add to any green salad for texture and flavor. Spinach salad, hot or cold, is incomplete without them.

PEPPERS: Red or green strips of fresh pepper add crispness and color to salads. For an antipasto salad, roast some seeded red peppers in the oven; peel and marinate in oil and vinegar. Out of season, look for canned pimientos to add color to salads.

RADISHES: Another colorful salad vegetable, both red and white radishes have a stingy, zesty bite; slice to serve in salads. Serve whole as part of an hors d'oeuvre salad, to dip into cool creamy blue cheese dressing or dip.

TOMATOES: Essential to most salads and perfect when sliced and simply dressed with herb vinaigrette. Also use as a salad container: Hollow out tomatoes, drain very well and fill with lentil salad, three-bean salad or rice salad.

ZUCCHINI: An excellent alternative to cucumber; slice young, unpeeled zucchini thinly and toss with sliced mushrooms for a raw vegetable salad. Or hollow out zucchini and fill with ham, tongue or potato salad.

GO-WITHS

ANCHOVIES: Flavorful and salty, anchovies are available in many forms: in fillets, rolled around capers, or as a paste. Use whole in salad antipasto, slice finely and toss with traditional Caesar salad; use the paste to give a hint of flavor to a seafood dressing.

BACON: Crisply fried, crumbled bacon is the perfect salad topping; use in spinach salad, potato salad or sprinkle lavishly over a sliced tomato or mushroom salad.

BLUE CHEESE: Crumbled blue cheese is best in a spinach or romaine lettuce salad; because of the strong flavor of blue cheese, use sparingly. Use in tiny wedges with raw mushrooms on a bed of watercress sprigs, or stir into sour cream dressing.

CROUTONS: Make your own from day-old bread and sauté in olive oil or bacon fat until crisp, flavoring the oil with garlic, if desired. Or, toss the cooked croutons with grated Parmesan cheese or dried herbs; always store in an airtight jar in the refrigerator.

DRIED FRUIT: A deliciously different, and often nutritious salad addition. Try dried raisins, snipped dates, slivers of dried apricots, apples or figs, and pieces of dried pineapple.

NUTS AND SEEDS: Walnuts are good with fruit salads and are traditional in Waldorf salad; try them, also, in potato salad. Pecans go well in citrus-based salads. Peanuts, cashews and pistachios make salty, crunchy toppings. Toasted pumpkin and sunflower seeds or sesame seeds are good, too.

OLIVES: Salty or mild, whole or sliced, black or green, pitted or stuffed, the tangy flavor of olives is a must in a feta cheese salad and all antipasto salads; try them in citrus salads and in mild vegetable salads.

ONIONS: A little onion goes a long way; raw and freshly chopped, it is perfect for vegetable salads, salad relishes and sharp dressings. Crisp onions in cans are a pleasant topping for simple lettuce, tomato and cucumber salads.

DRESSINGS

BASIC VINAIGRETTE: ¼ cup olive or vegetable oil, 2 tablespoons red wine, cider or tarragon vinegar, ½ teaspoon each salt, dry mustard and sugar, ⅛ teaspoon pepper, 1 small clove garlic, crushed. Combine and shake in screw-top jar; chill.

BASIC MAYONNAISE: 1 egg yolk, 2 tablespoons lemon juice or cider vinegar, ½ teaspoon each dry mustard and salt, 3 to 4 drops hot pepper sauce, 1 cup olive or vegetable oil. Combine all ingredients except oil in blender; slowly blend in oil at high speed, 1 or 2 drops at a time; chill.

HERB VINAIGRETTE: To basic vinaigrette, add 2 tablespoons chopped fresh parsley, basil or dill weed; or use chopped watercress, celery leaves or mint leaves. Or use dried herbs instead, approximately ½ teaspoon of each variety.

ITALIAN DRESSING: Double volume of basic vinaigrette; add 1 tablespoon each finely chopped red pepper, green pepper and onion, ½ teaspoon each dried basil, oregano and mild paprika.

LOUIS DRESSING: To basic mayonnaise, add ¼ cup each sour cream, chili sauce, finely chopped green pepper and green onion, 1 tablespoon lemon juice and 1 teaspoon grated lemon rind. Serve with crabmeat salad.

RUSSIAN DRESSING: To basic mayonnaise, add ¼ cup each chili sauce and finely chopped pimiento, 1 finely chopped hard-cooked egg, 1 tablespoon snipped chives, 1 tablespoon lemon juice, 1 teaspoon each grated lemon rind and paprika.

SOUR CREAM: A good on-hand ingredient for instant salad dressing. Add any of the following: crumbled blue cheese, crumbled fried bacon, finely chopped onion, fresh dill, honey, lemon juice, lemon rind. Perfect for potato salad or fruit salad.

YOGURT: For a low-fat, low-calorie alternative to sour cream, try yogurt; it is best when flavored with chopped mint, grated lemon rind, chopped fresh parsley, dill or basil. Good with beets, cucumbers, mushroom or tomato salads.

FAST-FOOD FEASTS

Fast foods, originally considered a boon to busy working people, now have another advantage: They can save kitchen energy as well as your own energy. By picking up some take-out food on the way home, to be featured as the main dish of an "instant" menu, you may save more than an hour of cooking energy.

All you need do is follow the accompanying menus and work plans. It's simple to create a fast-food feast for four or more if you remember these points.

- Take-out foods invariably cool down before they reach the table. A little reheating will restore crispness and appetite appeal; a little seasoning will restore and amplify flavor. Whenever possible, add a simple sauce or topping such as those used in Herbed Fish Bake, Taco Bake and Zesty Pork Chops.
- Carefully follow the reheating instructions in the work plan. Take-out food has already been cooked once, so it is usually best to wrap it in heavy-duty aluminum foil to retain moisture and flavor while reheating.
- The trimmings (rice, potatoes, bread) that often accompany take-out food can be just reheated, or a new herb or spice can be added, or you can use these trimmings to form the basis of an effortless side dish. Try Potato-Corn Scallop with the Pork

Dinner or try Ginger Rice with the Oriental Beef Dinner.

• Take-out foods usually need the addition of a vegetable dish, sometimes a salad and always a dessert. Choose side dishes that use convenience foods and can be quickly prepared while the main dish is reheating, perhaps even cooking the side dish alongside the main dish in the oven. For example, steak sandwiches reheat as the Hot Macaroni Salad and Quick Cherry Crisp are baking, and fried chicken reheats as the Broiled Parmesan Potatoes and Spiced Peaches are cooking, as outlined in two menus in this chapter.

• Choose accompanying salads with ingredients that are thinly sliced and quickly chilled. Have desserts that are made ahead with a minimum of energy expenditure, or are instantly devised at the last moment from a swirl of ice cream and a lavish helping of fruit and prepared sauce.

Use the work plans as well as the menus to achieve true energy efficiency. Most of these menus are prepared entirely in the oven; if only the main dish needs reheating, use a toaster oven or top-of-the-stove heat to conserve energy.

Fast-food feasts can be work efficient, time efficient and energy efficient. With the simple recipes and tips that follow, fast-food feasts are also delicious.

ORIENTAL BEEF DINNER

EGG ROLLS

BOURLOU GAI PAN PLUS*

GINGER RICE*

HAWAIIAN TORTE*

TROPICAL PUNCH*

Serves 4.

WORK PLAN: Purchase egg rolls with sauce (enough for 4 as an appetizer) and bourlou gai pan with rice (enough for 4 as a main course) from a franchise Chinese restaurant. Prepare Hawaiian Torte. Prepare Ginger Rice and Bourlou Gai Pan Plus. Ten minutes before torte is done, reheat egg rolls in oven; serve with sauce as an appetizer. Make Tropical Punch at last moment.

HAWAIIAN TORTE

one 13½-ounce package spicy apple-raisin snack cake mix
one 8-ounce can crushed pineapple

½ cup water
½ cup flaked coconut

1. Preheat oven to 375° F. In large bowl of electric mixer, combine cake mix, *undrained* pineapple and water. Beat on medium speed until thoroughly blended.

2. Pour batter into a greased and floured 8-inch round baking dish (3 inches high). Sprinkle with coconut.

3. Bake 25 to 30 minutes. Serve warm, either plain or with ice cream. *Serves 6.*

GINGER RICE

4 portions cooked rice
1 tablespoon chopped parsley

1 tablespoon finely chopped candied ginger

1. Place rice in top part of double boiler over simmering water.

2. Stir in parsley and ginger. Cover and heat until rice is heated through.

BOURLOU GAI PAN PLUS

4 portions bourlou gai pan (beef strips in vegetable sauce)   **one 10-ounce package frozen Chinese-style vegetables with sauce, thawed**

1. Turn the bourlou gai pan into a large shallow skillet. Stir in the thawed Chinese vegetables with sauce; mix well.

2. Simmer over moderate heat until just at boiling point. Serve with Ginger Rice.

TROPICAL PUNCH

2 cups grapefruit juice, chilled   **one 8-ounce bottle ginger ale or club soda, chilled**
2 cups apricot nectar, chilled

1. In a large pitcher, mix grapefruit juice and apricot nectar.

2. When ready to serve, add chilled ginger ale or club soda. Stir and serve at once over ice in tall glasses.

For an alternate menu, try:

EGG ROLLS WITH
SHERRY-SOY SAUCE

BOURLOU GAI PAN PLUS

RICE AND BEAN SPROUTS

LIME-COCONUT DESSERT

Use the same work plan, with the following changes:

Dessert
Divide a pint of lime sherbet, one 8-ounce can crushed pineapple, and ½ cup flaked coconut among 4 parfait glasses in layers.

Rice
Prepare rice as directed in recipe, omitting ginger; stir in 1 cup canned bean sprouts, rinsed and drained.

Appetizer
Heat egg rolls as directed. To accompanying soy sauce, add ¼ cup dry sherry, 1 small clove garlic, crushed, and ½ teaspoon powdered ginger.

STEAK DINNER

STEAK

SALAD

SPINACH TOMATOES *

CHEESE BREAD *

CHOCOLATE CREAM CAKE *

Serves 4.

WORK PLAN: Purchase 4 steak dinners with salad from franchise pancake and steak restaurant. Prepare Chocolate Cream Cake. Prepare Cheese Bread and Spinach Tomatoes; bake both on top shelf of oven. Ten minutes before bread and tomatoes are done, place steak in 13 x 9 x 2-inch baking dish; cover and reheat in oven. Serve with salad.

CHOCOLATE CREAM CAKE

one 9-inch store-bought angel food cake
1 cup heavy cream
¼ cup sugar

2 tablespoons unsweetened cocoa powder
½ teaspoon vanilla extract
chocolate sprinkles

1. Split angel food cake into 3 round layers; brush off loose crumbs.

2. Beat heavy cream until it begins to thicken, gradually adding a mixture of the sugar and the cocoa powder.

3. Continue to beat cream, adding vanilla extract, until stiff.

4. Fill and frost layers and top of cake. Sprinkle with chocolate sprinkles. *Serves 8 to 10.*

CHEESE BREAD

2 large French rolls
¼ cup butter or margarine

¼ cup grated Parmesan cheese
2 tablespoons finely chopped parsley

1. Split each roll lengthwise and place on baking sheet.

2. Mix butter or margarine, cheese and parsley. Spread over cut side of each halved roll. Bake at 350° F for about 25 minutes until hot and crisp.

SPINACH TOMATOES

4 medium-size ripe tomatoes
one 10-ounce package frozen chopped
**   spinach, thawed and drained**
2 tablespoons mayonnaise

¼ teaspoon salt
¼ cup dry seasoned bread crumbs
2 teaspoons butter or margarine

1. Halve the tomatoes and arrange cut side up in greased shallow baking dish.

2. Press thawed spinach in a strainer or colander to remove all moisture. In small bowl, mix spinach, mayonnaise and salt.

3. Mound spinach mixture on top of tomatoes and sprinkle with bread crumbs. Add a dot of butter or margarine to each tomato half and bake at 350° F for about 20 minutes.

For an alternate menu, try:

STEAK

SALAD

OVEN-BAKED ONIONS
AND CARROTS

CHEESE BREAD

CHOCOLATE CREAM SHORTCAKE

Use the same work plan, with the following changes:

Dessert
Place a large scoop of chocolate ice cream in each of 4 individual sponge cake shells; freeze. At serving time, frost with Chocolate Cream (see recipe for Chocolate Cream Cake) and chocolate sprinkles.

Vegetables
In 13 x 9 x 2-inch baking dish, combine one 16-ounce can each whole onions and whole baby carrots, drained. Add ¼ cup butter or margarine, 1 teaspoon each salt and basil, and ¼ teaspoon pepper. Heat, covered, alongside cheese bread.

STEAK SANDWICH DINNER

STEAK SANDWICHES

SAUCY CARROT SLICES*

HOT MACARONI SALAD*

QUICK CHERRY CRISP*

Serves 4.

WORK PLAN: Purchase 4 steak sandwiches with onion topping from a franchise food store. Prepare Saucy Carrot Slices and chill as directed. Prepare Quick Cherry Crisp and bake in upper third of oven. Prepare Hot Macaroni Salad and bake in bottom third of oven. Wrap each steak sandwich in heavy-duty aluminum foil; reheat alongside macaroni salad.

SAUCY CARROT SLICES

2 cups thinly sliced carrots   **½ cup bottled French dressing**

1. In medium saucepan, bring carrots and salted water to cover to boiling point. Reduce heat and simmer for 5 minutes.

2. Drain carrots, then add dressing; toss well. Chill until ready to serve.

Note: To speed chilling process, set carrots in freezer for no longer than 30 minutes.

QUICK CHERRY CRISP

one 12-ounce package oatmeal cookie mix
1 egg

1 cup cherry preserves
stiffly beaten heavy cream or refrigerator dessert topping

1. Preheat oven to 350° F.

2. Thoroughly combine cookie mix and egg. Press half the mixture firmly and evenly into lightly greased 8-inch square baking pan. Spread with preserves. Sprinkle remaining cookie mix over preserves. Press down lightly.

3. Bake 35 to 40 minutes, until cookie topping is crisp and the filling is bubbly. Cool on wire rack for 5 minutes. Serve warm with whipped cream or whipped topping. *Serves 4 to 6.*

HOT MACARONI SALAD

1½ cups uncooked elbow macaroni
2 tablespoons finely chopped green
  pepper
1 teaspoon Dijon-style mustard
1 tablespoon finely chopped fresh parsley
  or 1 teaspoon dried parsley

½ teaspoon salt
2 or 3 drops hot pepper sauce
⅓ cup mayonnaise

1. Cook macaroni according to label directions. Drain; turn into large bowl.

2. Add green pepper, mustard, parsley, salt and hot pepper sauce; mix well. Blend in mayonnaise. If mixture appears too dry, blend in an additional 1 or 2 tablespoons mayonnaise or sour cream.

3. Turn mixture into 1½-quart casserole. Bake at 350° F for about 10 to 15 minutes or until heated through.

Note: This dish can also be served cold.

For an alternate menu, try:

STEAK SANDWICHES

GREEN BEANS VINAIGRETTE

HOT MACARONI SALAD

CHERRY TRIFLE

Use the same work plan, with the following changes:

Vegetables
Drain two 16-ounce cans cut green beans; toss with ½ cup bottled French dressing and ¼ cup chopped parsley. Chill as directed for Saucy Carrot Slices.

Dessert
Cut one 9-ounce frozen pound cake, thawed, into thin slices; sandwich together with cherry preserves, then cut into ½-inch cubes. Place in bottom of 1½-quart serving bowl; sprinkle with ¼ cup sherry and top with one 20-ounce can cherry pie filling. Chill and served topped with 1 cup heavy cream, stiffly beaten.

ROAST BEEF DINNER

HOT ROAST BEEF SANDWICHES

CHILI TOMATOES*

SPROUTED POTATO SALAD*

FRUITS IN YOGURT*

Serves 4.

WORK PLAN: Purchase 4 roast beef sandwiches from a franchise food store (or delicatessen). Prepare Fruits in Yogurt. Make Sprouted Potato Salad and Chili Tomatoes. Wrap each sandwich in heavy-duty aluminum foil; set in oven to reheat while tomatoes are broiling, or set in toaster oven at 350° F for 15 minutes.

FRUITS IN YOGURT

one 17-ounce can chunky fruits for fruit salad

1 unpeeled apple, diced
one 8-ounce container raspberry yogurt

1. Partially drain chunky fruits; turn fruits into serving dish or bowl. Stir in diced apple.

2. Stir yogurt to distribute raspberry preserves throughout yogurt. Spoon over fruits in serving dish. Chill until ready to serve.

Note: If desired, drain chunky fruits completely for a less juicy dessert.

SPROUTED POTATO SALAD

1 pint store-bought potato salad
½ cup alfalfa sprouts

2 tablespoons bottled Italian dressing
parsley sprigs

1. Turn potato salad into serving bowl. Mix in ¼ cup of the alfalfa sprouts and the Italian dressing.

2. Garnish around edge of bowl with remaining alfalfa sprouts and a few sprigs of parsley.

CHILI TOMATOES

one 14½-ounce can stewed tomatoes
1 tablespoon chopped fresh parsley, or
  1½ teaspoons dried parsley
¼ teaspoon salt

¼ teaspoon chili powder
1 tablespoon butter or margarine
2 tablespoons dry bread crumbs
2 tablespoons grated Parmesan cheese

1. Preheat broiler.

2. Pour stewed tomatoes into well-greased 8-inch square baking dish. Stir in parsley, salt and chili powder.

3. Dot with butter or margarine, sprinkle with bread crumbs mixed with grated cheese. Broil 4 inches from heat for 5 or 6 minutes, until brown on top and bubbly hot.

For an alternate menu, try:

HOT ROAST BEEF SANDWICHES

SAVORY BACON POTATOES

APPLE SALAD

ICE CREAM SHELLS WITH FRUIT

Use the same work plan, with the following changes:

Dessert
Using 1½ pints vanilla ice cream, press over bottom and sides of four 6-ounce custard cups to form ⅓-inch-thick shells. Freeze until serving time; fill with one 17-ounce can chunky fruits for fruit salad, drained.

Salad
Toss 2 cups thinly sliced tart apples (peeled) with ¼ cup herb salad dressing and 2 teaspoons dried mint; chill.

Vegetables
Fry 6 slices bacon in heatproof casserole on top of stove. Crumble bacon, then add two 16-ounce cans potatoes, drained and sliced. Heat, adding ¼ cup red wine vinegar, 1 teaspoon salt and ¼ teaspoon pepper. Place in oven to keep hot while reheating roast beef sandwiches.

SIRLOINER DINNER

CHEESE SIRLOINERS

BARBECUED FRENCH FRIES*

CUCUMBER COLESLAW*

MOCHA FLUFF PIE*

Serves 4.

WORK PLAN: A few hours before dinner, prepare Mocha Fluff Pie and freeze as directed. Purchase 4 cheese sirloiners from a franchise food store. Prepare Cucumber Coleslaw and chill. Make Barbecued French Fries. Ten minutes before fries are done, wrap each cheeseburger in heavy-duty aluminum foil; place in oven to reheat.

MOCHA FLUFF PIE

one 8-ounce container coffee yogurt
one 4½-ounce container refrigerator
    dessert topping
⅓ cup chocolate syrup

2 tablespoons sugar
one 9-inch prepared graham cracker pie
    shell

1. In large bowl, gently fold together yogurt, whipped topping, ¼ cup of the chocolate syrup and the sugar. Spoon into prepared pie shell.

2. Garnish top of pie with several zigzag strips of the remaining chocolate syrup. Freeze for 2 to 3 hours, until firm. *Serves 6.*

Note: For a hurry-up version, prepare yogurt mixture, using all of chocolate syrup; spoon into 5 or 6 sherbet glasses or dessert dishes and sprinkle with graham cracker crumbs. Chill for about 20 minutes.

CUCUMBER COLESLAW

1 pint store-bought coleslaw
½ cup thinly sliced cucumber
⅓ cup mayonnaise

1 teaspoon sugar
3 or 4 drops hot pepper sauce
1 teaspoon mild paprika

1. In medium bowl, combine coleslaw and cucumber.

2. Add mayonnaise, sugar and hot pepper sauce. Toss ingredients together until well mixed. Cover with plastic wrap and chill.

3. Sprinkle with paprika before serving.

BARBECUED FRENCH FRIES

one 24-ounce polybag frozen steak fries   **1 tablespoon seasoned salt**

1. Preheat oven to 450° F.

2. Spread fries in single layer on large baking sheet. Sprinkle fries with seasoned salt. Bake for 15 minutes.

3. Using wide spatula, turn fries, then bake 15 minutes longer.

For an alternate menu, try:

CHEESE SIRLOINERS

MEXICAN-STYLE POTATOES

TOMATO-BEAN SALAD

ORANGE AND LEMON PIE

Use the same work plan, with the following changes:

Dessert

Slightly soften 1 quart lemon sherbet; stir in ½ cup bitter orange marmalade. Spoon into one 9-inch prepared graham cracker pie shell. Freeze until serving time; serve with unflavored yogurt as a topping.

Salad

Hollow out and drain 4 large tomatoes; fill with 1 pint store-bought three-bean salad. Chill until serving time.

Vegetables

Heat 2 tablespoons vegetable oil in large metal baking pan in 450° F oven; add two 16-ounce cans whole tiny potatoes, well drained. Sprinkle with 1 tablespoon seasoned salt and 1 to 1½ teaspoons chili powder. Heat 15 minutes, stirring frequently.

Reheat cheeseburgers during the last 10 minutes, as directed.

TACO DINNER

TACO BAKE*

SPINACH SALAD*

MERINGUE PEACHES*

Serves 6.

WORK PLAN: Purchase 6 tacos from a franchise restaurant specializing in Mexican food. Prepare Spinach Salad; chill. Make Taco Bake. Prepare Meringue Peaches and bake during dinner.

SPINACH SALAD

1 pound fresh spinach
1 cup sliced fresh mushrooms
½ cup unflavored yogurt

½ teaspoon sugar
¼ teaspoon celery salt

1. Rinse spinach and remove stems. Pat spinach dry, then tear leaves into a salad bowl. Add the sliced mushrooms.

2. In a small screwtop jar, combine yogurt, sugar and celery salt. Shake until well mixed. If dressing is too thick, add 2 tablespoons vinegar, milk or vegetable juice.

3. Chill salad and dressing. When ready to serve, pour dressing over salad and toss well.

TACO BAKE

6 tacos (toasted tortilla shells with a filling of chili-seasoned ground beef, topped with shredded cheese, shredded lettuce and chopped tomato)

one 16-ounce can chili with beans
one 16-ounce can tomato sauce
2 cups grated Monterey Jack or longhorn cheese

1. Preheat oven to 400° F. Overlap tacos in a greased 12 x 8 x 2-inch baking dish.

2. Spoon chili with beans over tacos; pour tomato sauce over all. Sprinkle cheese in an even layer on top.

3. Bake 30 minutes, or until mixture bubbles and cheese browns.

MERINGUE PEACHES

2 egg whites
¼ teaspoon cream of tartar
dash of salt
½ cup sugar

6 canned or fresh peach halves
6 whole strawberries or walnut halves
shredded coconut

1. Preheat oven to 350° F. In small bowl, beat egg whites with cream of tartar and dash of salt until foamy.

2. Gradually add sugar, beating continuously until stiff peaks form.

3. Arrange peach halves hollow side up in 8-inch baking dish. Place strawberry or walnut half in each hollow. Cover peach with mound of meringue; sprinkle with coconut. Bake 10 to 12 minutes, or until puffed and brown.

For an alternate menu, try:

TACO BAKE

CELERY SLAW

STUFFED APRICOTS
IN ORANGE SAUCE

Use the same work plan, with the following changes:

Salad

Cut 8 to 10 celery stalks to measure 4 cups thin julienne strips; stir in ¼ cup each unflavored yogurt, sour cream and chopped celery leaves, 1 teaspoon salt, and 4 to 6 drops hot pepper sauce.

Dessert

Drain one 32-ounce can whole apricots, reserving juice; remove pits, keeping apricots whole. Blend together ½ cup each shredded coconut and ground almonds; add a little apricot juice to permit mixture to be rolled into balls. Fill center of each apricot with a coconut-almond ball. Place stuffed apricots in 13 x 9 x 2-inch baking dish. Pour over a mixture of ½ cup orange marmalade and the remaining apricot juice. Bake alongside Taco Bake. Serve with ice cream, if desired.

PORK DINNER

ZESTY PORK CHOPS*

POTATO-CORN SCALLOP*

TOSSED SALAD

BAKED MARMALADE APPLES*

Serves 4.

WORK PLAN: Purchase 4 franchise pork chop dinners, each containing 2 pork chops, a serving of hash browns and tossed salad. Prepare Zesty Pork Chops, Potato-Corn Scallop and Baked Marmalade Apples; bake potatoes and apples in top third of oven and pork chops in bottom third. Place tossed salad on 4 salad dishes and chill until serving time; serve with dressing included in franchise dinner.

ZESTY PORK CHOPS

8 cooked pork chops
1 beef bouillon cube

½ cup hot water
1 teaspoon Dijon-style mustard

1. Arrange chops in lightly greased 12 x 8 x 2-inch baking dish, overlapping if necessary.

2. Mix bouillon cube in ½ cup hot water until dissolved. Stir in mustard. Pour mixture over chops. Cover dish tightly with foil; bake at 400° F for about 35 minutes.

POTATO-CORN SCALLOP

one 16-ounce can cream-style corn
4 portions hash brown potatoes
¼ cup chopped green pepper
½ teaspoon salt

2 or 3 drops hot pepper sauce
1 tablespoon butter or margarine
½ cup soft fresh bread crumbs

1. Mix together corn, hash browns, green pepper, salt and hot pepper sauce. Pour into lightly greased 1½-quart casserole.

2. Dot with butter or margarine and sprinkle with bread crumbs. Bake at 400° F for about 35 minutes, until browned and bubbly. *Serves 4 to 6.*

BAKED MARMALADE APPLES

4 medium apples
2 tablespoons sugar
½ cup orange marmalade

1 teaspoon cinnamon
¼ teaspoon nutmeg

1. Core and halve apples horizontally. Arrange apples cut side up in lightly greased 8-inch baking dish.

2. Sprinkle apples with sugar, spread with marmalade and sprinkle with cinnamon and nutmeg. Cover and bake at 400° F for about 35 minutes.

For an alternate menu, try:

ZESTY PORK CHOPS

OVEN-FRIED ONIONS
AND HASH BROWNS

TOSSED SALAD

APPLE-DATE CRISP

Use the same work plan, with the following changes:

Vegetables
In a large skillet over medium heat, sauté 3 cups thinly sliced onion rings and 1 cup chopped green pepper in 2 tablespoons vegetable oil until tender. Add 1 teaspoon salt and ¼ teaspoon pepper; crumble in 4 portions hash brown potatoes. Place in 1½-quart heatproof casserole and bake in 400° F oven for about 35 minutes.

Dessert
In 8 x 8 x 2-inch baking dish, place 4 cups thinly sliced ripe pears (peeled), ¼ cup chopped dates and 2 tablespoons each brown sugar and lemon juice. Top with 2 cups crushed oatmeal cookies; dot with 2 tablespoons butter or margarine. Bake in 400° F oven for about 35 minutes.

BARBECUED RIB DINNER

BUCKET OF RIBS

FRIED BEANS*

COUNTRY SLAW*

DOUBLE LEMON PUDDING*

Serves 4.

WORK PLAN: Purchase one medium-size bucket of barbecued pork ribs from a franchise rib and chicken store. Prepare Double Lemon Pudding and Country Slaw. Spread barbecued ribs in 15 x 10 x 2-inch baking pan and reheat at 400° F for about 15 minutes. Meanwhile, prepare Fried Beans.

DOUBLE LEMON PUDDING

one 3¾-ounce package instant lemon
  pudding
2½ cups cold milk

1 cup lemon yogurt
8 gingersnaps, crumbled

1. Prepare instant pudding according to label directions, using 2½ cups cold milk. Add lemon yogurt; stir until smooth.

2. Divide crumbled gingersnaps among 4 sherbet glasses or dishes, reserving some for garnish. Press crumbs to bottom and sides of glasses.

3. Stir pudding and spoon into glasses. Sprinkle with reserved gingersnap crumbs and chill until serving time.

COUNTRY SLAW

4 cups shredded cabbage (½ small head)
¾ cup grated carrot
⅓ cup vegetable oil
¼ cup vinegar
3 tablespoons mayonnaise

1 teaspoon horseradish
½ teaspoon salt
½ teaspoon sugar
¼ teaspoon celery salt

1. In salad bowl, combine cabbage and carrot.

2. In large screwtop jar, combine oil, vinegar, mayonnaise, horseradish, salt, sugar and celery salt. Shake vigorously until dressing is blended and smooth.

3. Pour dressing over salad; toss lightly until well mixed. Chill until ready to serve.

FRIED BEANS

2 tablespoons vegetable oil
¼ cup chopped onion
one 21-ounce can baked beans
2 tablespoons ketchup

1 tablespoon sweet pickle relish
1 teaspoon prepared mustard
1 tablespoon vinegar (optional)

1. Heat oil in large skillet over medium heat; add onion and sauté until tender, about 5 minutes. Reduce heat to medium-low; stir in beans, ketchup, relish and mustard.

2. Simmer beans for 10 minutes, stirring frequently. For extra tang and flavor, stir in vinegar before serving.

For an alternate menu, try:

BUCKET OF RIBS

BACON CORN MUFFINS

DOWN-HOME TOMATO SALAD

INDIVIDUAL APPLE PIES

Use the same work plan, with the following changes:

Salad
Slice 4 large tomatoes thinly; arrange on shallow lettuce-lined dish in overlapping lines. Sprinkle with 1 teaspoon each sugar, salt and basil; sprinkle with ¼ cup oil and vinegar dressing. Chill.

Corn Muffins
Prepare one 8-ounce package corn muffin mix according to label directions, adding 2 tablespoons crumbled bacon bits and ½ teaspoon cracked or ground black pepper. Bake on top shelf of 400° F oven for 15 to 20 minutes.

Dessert
Roll buttermilk biscuits from one 8-ounce package into 10 circles, as thin as possible. Place 3 to 4 tablespoons prepared apple pie filling on top of each of 5 circles; press remaining 5 circles on top, dampening edges to seal. Bake on top shelf of 400° F oven for 15 to 20 minutes.

Reheat ribs on lower shelf of oven for about 15 minutes.

PIZZA DINNER

PIZZA WITH FIX-UPS*

ITALIAN SALAD*

POSH STRAWBERRY SUNDAES*

Serves 4.

WORK PLAN: Purchase one 14-inch cheese pizza from a take-out pizza store. Make Italian Salad. Prepare Posh Strawberry Sundaes, then Pizza with Fix-Ups. *(Dinner shown on page 86.)*

ITALIAN SALAD

½ **pound green beans**
1 **cucumber, thinly sliced**
1 **small onion, thinly sliced**
⅓ **cup vegetable or olive oil**
¼ **cup vinegar**
½ **teaspoon salt**
½ **teaspoon oregano**

¼ **teaspoon celery salt**
¼ **teaspoon garlic salt**
¼ **teaspoon dry mustard**
celery sticks
pimiento strips
ripe olives

1. Rinse and trim green beans, but leave whole. Boil beans in water to cover for 6 minutes, until crisp-tender. Drain and chill for 45 to 60 minutes.

2. Layer cucumber, onion and beans in salad bowl.

3. In screwtop jar, combine oil, vinegar, salt, oregano, celery salt, garlic salt and dry mustard. Shake well to blend. Pour over vegetables in bowl. Chill until ready to serve. Garnish with celery sticks, pimiento strips and ripe olives.

Note: To speed chilling process, set green beans in freezer for no longer than 30 minutes.

POSH STRAWBERRY SUNDAES

1 **cup strawberry jam or sundae topping**
2 **tablespoons orange juice**
1 **tablespoon anise- or orange-flavored liqueur**

1½ **pints vanilla ice cream**
refrigerator dessert topping (optional)
chocolate sprinkles (optional)

1. Mix jam or sundae topping with orange juice and liqueur. Stir until completely blended.

2. Spoon sauce over scoops of vanilla ice cream in 4 sherbet glasses. Freeze until serving time. Top with whipped topping and sprinkles if desired.

PIZZA WITH FIX-UPS

one 14-inch ready-to-eat cheese pizza
one of the following Fix-ups:

FIX-UP 1
¼ **pound sliced boiled ham, cut into**
    julienne strips
¼ **pound thinly sliced provolone cheese,**
    cut into julienne strips
½ **cup sliced stuffed olives**

FIX-UP 2
¼ **pound thinly sliced pepperoni or salami**
1 **cup shredded mozzarella cheese**
⅓ **cup sliced black olives**

FIX-UP 3
½ **pound ground beef or sausage meat**
1 **cup grated longhorn cheese**
¼ **cup chopped green pepper**

FIX-UP 4
6 **frankfurters, thinly sliced**
1 **small onion, thinly sliced**
1 **cup grated American cheese**

TOPPING
one 8-ounce can tomato sauce
½ **teaspoon oregano**
salt and pepper to taste
red pepper flakes to taste (optional)

1. Preheat oven to 400° F. Place pizza on cookie sheet or pizza pan.

2. Top pizza with one of the Fix-ups. (If using Fix-up 3, sauté ground beef or sausage meat in medium skillet over medium heat until well done, breaking meat into small pieces with fork; spread over pizza along with other Fix-up ingredients.)

3. For topping, spoon tomato sauce over all; sprinkle with oregano, salt and pepper, and red pepper flakes if desired.

4. Bake for 10 minutes or until pizza is heated through and cheese is melted.

EnergySaving Tip: A ready-to-eat pizza, whether from your local pizza store or from the freezer of your supermarket, can be fixed up in many ways. One of the Fix-ups (above) can be used to top the entire pizza; if you wish, make all four Fix-ups and use part of each one to top a quarter of the pizza. Place each leftover Fix-up in an airtight container and freeze for later use. Other Fix-ups to place on top of a pizza, either singly or in combination, are:
• 1½ cups each julienne strips green and red pepper, sautéed until crisp-tender in 2 tablespoons olive oil and seasoned with ½ teaspoon each salt and oregano, and ¼ teaspoon red pepper flakes.
• 3 cups thinly sliced mushrooms (about ½ pound), sautéed in 2 tablespoons vegetable oil until just tender; stir in ½ cup sliced stuffed olives, 2 tablespoons lemon juice, ½ teaspoon salt and ¼ teaspoon pepper.
• 2 cups thinly sliced onion rings, sautéed in 1 tablespoon vegetable oil and seasoned with ½ teaspoon salt and ⅛ teaspoon pepper; drain and set aside. In same skillet, sauté 2 cups of ⅓-inch-thick tomato slices until just tender; drain and sprinkle with ½ teaspoon each salt and basil leaves. Arrange evenly over surface of pizza, alternating with onion rings.

SUBMARINE DINNER

SUBMARINE SANDWICHES

TOMATO-MINIE SOUP*

RELISHES

SICILIAN APRICOTS*

Serves 4.

WORK PLAN: Purchase 4 over-stuffed submarine (hero) sandwiches from a delicatessen. Prepare Sicilian Apricots; chill. Arrange 1 cup each celery and carrot sticks and strips of sour pickles on large platter; cover and chill relishes until serving time. Make Tomato-Minie Soup. Place submarine sandwiches on large serving platter; garnish with thinly sliced onions and parsley.

SICILIAN APRICOTS

one 17-ounce can apricot halves
1 cup ricotta cheese
¼ cup chopped maraschino cherries
2 tablespoons miniature chocolate
  morsels

2 tablespoons sugar
1 teaspoon grated orange rind
⅛ teaspoon salt

1. In each of 4 sherbet glasses, arrange 2 or 3 apricot halves hollow side up. Reserve 4 apricot halves for garnish.

2. In a medium bowl, mix cheese, cherries, chocolate morsels, sugar, orange rind and salt. Divide mixture into 4 parts and spoon over apricots.

3. Top each serving with a reserved apricot half.

TOMATO-MINIE SOUP

one 10½-ounce can condensed
  minestrone soup
one 10½-ounce can condensed tomato
  soup

¼ cup chopped parsley
½ teaspoon oregano
2½ cups water

1. In a large saucepan, combine condensed minestrone and condensed tomato soup, chopped parsley and oregano; mix well.

2. Stir in water. Heat to boiling point and serve in big mugs. *Serves 4 to 6.*

FRIED CHICKEN DINNER

FRIED CHICKEN

BROILED PARMESAN POTATOES
AND SPICED PEACHES*

SOUR CREAM-BEAN SALAD*

LEMON SHERBET

Serves 4.

WORK PLAN: Purchase one economy box of 9 fried chicken pieces from a franchise chicken store. For dessert, divide 1½ pints lemon sherbet among 4 dessert dishes; sprinkle each serving with 1 tablespoon grated semisweet chocolate, and freeze until serving time. Prepare Sour Cream-Bean Salad. Prepare Broiled Parmesan Potatoes and Spiced Peaches; place fried chicken in 15 x 10 x 2-inch baking pan; reheat in oven while potatoes are broiling.

SOUR CREAM-BEAN SALAD

one 16-ounce can cut green beans, drained
1 cup sliced celery
1 cup sour cream

½ teaspoon dried dill
½ teaspoon sugar
salt and pepper to taste

1. Place drained green beans in serving bowl. Add sliced celery, sour cream, dill, sugar, salt and pepper.

2. Toss until thoroughly mixed. Chill until ready to serve.

BROILED PARMESAN POTATOES AND SPICED PEACHES

one 16-ounce can sliced white potatoes, drained
2 tablespoons butter or margarine
2 tablespoons grated Parmesan cheese

one 16-ounce can peach halves, drained
¼ cup sugar
¼ teaspoon cinnamon

1. Preheat broiler.

2. Arrange drained potatoes in single layer on broiler pan. Dot with 1 tablespoon of the butter or margarine and sprinkle with grated cheese.

3. Arrange drained peaches rounded side up on broiler pan with potatoes. Broil 3 to 4 inches from heat for 4 minutes.

4. Turn peaches hollow side up. Dot peaches with remaining butter or margarine; sprinkle with mixture of sugar and cinnamon. Broil 4 minutes longer, or until potatoes and peaches are browned.

CANTON CHICKEN DINNER

BARBECUED SPARERIBS

TOMATO SAUCE*

MUSTARD SAUCE*

BONELESS CHICKEN CANTONESE

RICE

STIR-FRY PEA PODS*

POLYNESIAN PIE*

CHINESE TEA

Serves 4.

WORK PLAN: Prepare Polynesian Pie and chill until dessert time (or prepare and chill overnight). Purchase barbecued spareribs (as an appetizer for 4) and boneless chicken Cantonese (as a main course for 4) from a franchise Chinese restaurant. Place spareribs in large baking pan and reheat at 350° F for about 25 minutes. Place chicken in 2-quart casserole; cover and reheat alongside ribs. Meanwhile, cook 1 cup long-grain rice according to label directions. Prepare Tomato Sauce and Mustard Sauce; serve with ribs for first course. Just before serving up the chicken and rice, prepare Stir-Fry Pea Pods. Make some Chinese tea at last moment. *(Dinner shown on page 87.)*

POLYNESIAN PIE

one 4½-ounce package instant vanilla
  pudding
1 cup sour cream
one 8-ounce can mandarin oranges,
  drained

one 8-ounce can pineapple chunks,
  drained
one 9-inch prepared graham cracker pie
  shell
slivered almonds (optional)

1. In a medium bowl, prepare instant pudding according to label directions. As pudding begins to thicken, stir in sour cream.

2. Fold in well-drained mandarin oranges and pineapple.

3. Spoon pudding and fruit into prepared pie shell. Garnish with slivered almonds, if you wish. Chill several hours or until serving time. *Serves 6.*

TOMATO SAUCE

½ cup ketchup
2 or 3 tablespoons horseradish
2 tablespoons pickle relish
1 teaspoon lemon juice

3 or 4 drops hot pepper sauce
salt and pepper to taste
2 to 3 tablespoons sour cream (optional)

1. In a small bowl, mix ketchup, horseradish, relish, lemon juice and hot pepper sauce.

2. Taste and add salt and pepper if needed. For a creamy sauce, stir in 2 to 3 tablespoons sour cream. *Makes ¾ cup.*

MUSTARD SAUCE

2 tablespoons boiling water **1 teaspoon vegetable oil**
2 tablespoons dry mustard **¼ teaspoon salt**

1. In a small bowl, stir boiling water into dry mustard. Mix until smooth.

2. Stir in oil and salt. *Makes about ¼ cup.*

Note: For more sauce, double the ingredients; cover and store in refrigerator for a week or more, if desired.

STIR-FRY PEA PODS

2 tablespoons vegetable oil **½ cup sliced celery, cut on the diagonal**
one 9-ounce package frozen Chinese pea **salt and pepper to taste**
pods, thawed

1. Heat oil in a wok or skillet. Add pea pods and celery.

2. Stir and cook until vegetables are crisp-tender, about 5 to 7 minutes. Taste and add salt and pepper. Serve at once.

For an alternate dessert, try:

THREE SHERBET PIE WITH
CHESTNUT-GINGER SAUCE

Into one 9-inch prepared graham cracker pie shell, arrange tiny scoops of lemon, raspberry and lime sherbet. Arrange so that flavors are distributed throughout pie and pie mounds high; sprinkle with ¼ cup chopped crystallized ginger or ½ teaspoon powdered ginger; freeze.

Just before serving, combine 1 cup chestnut puree from one 16-ounce can chestnut puree, ½ cup maple syrup, ¼ cup chopped cyrstallized ginger (or ½ teaspoon powdered ginger) and 2 tablespoons brown sugar in medium saucepan. Heat, stirring constantly, but do not boil; serve warm alongside pie.

CREPE DINNER

CHICKEN DIVAN CREPES

GREEN BEANS

PINEAPPLE CRANBERRY SALAD*

SAVORY FRENCH BREAD

EASY ORANGE ICE CREAM*

BUTTER COOKIES

Serves 4 to 6.

WORK PLAN: The night before or at least 2 hours before serving, prepare Easy Orange Ice Cream; serve with butter cookies. Prepare Pineapple Cranberry Salad; chill. Purchase 8 to 12 chicken divan crêpes (chicken- and broccoli-stuffed crêpes) from a franchise crêpe restaurant. Place crêpes in a lightly greased 13 x 9 x 2-inch baking dish and cover with aluminum foil; reheat for 15 to 20 minutes at 350° F. Sprinkle top of a loaf of French bread with ¼ cup grated Parmesan cheese and ½ teaspoon powdered thyme; wrap in aluminum foil and heat alongside crêpes. Meanwhile, heat two 16-ounce cans whole green beans; toss with ¼ cup chopped black olives before serving.

EASY ORANGE ICE CREAM

1 quart vanilla ice cream
one 6-ounce can frozen orange juice
  concentrate, partially thawed

¼ cup orange-flavored liqueur, brandy or
  lemon juice

1. In a medium bowl, stir ice cream to soften. Stir in orange juice and orange-flavored liqueur, brandy or lemon juice. When well blended, pour into a 1-quart container.

2. Refreeze ice cream mixture until firm, at least 2 hours or preferably overnight.

PINEAPPLE CRANBERRY SALAD

lettuce leaves
one 20-ounce can sliced pineapple,
  drained

one 8-ounce can jellied cranberry sauce
½ cup mayonnaise
¼ cup chopped pecans or walnuts

1. Arrange lettuce leaves on 4 to 6 salad plates. Drain pineapple slices, reserving juice. Cut jellied cranberry sauce into 4 to 6 slices.

2. Place 2 pineapple slices on each lettuce-lined plate. Center a cranberry slice on top of the pineapple slices.

3. Blend mayonnaise with ¼ to ⅓ cup reserved pineapple juice. Chill dressing and salad. When ready to serve, spoon dressing over salad and sprinkle with chopped nuts.

CHOW MEIN DINNER

CHICKEN CHOW MEIN

CHINESE NOODLE NESTS*

GREEN BEANS WITH
WATER CHESTNUTS*

ORIENTAL FRUIT FREEZE*

Serves 4.

WORK PLAN: At least 1 hour before serving, prepare Oriental Fruit Freeze. Purchase chicken chow mein for 4 from a take-out Chinese restaurant; place in large saucepan and reheat over very low heat. Make Chinese Noodle Nests; keep warm while preparing Green Beans with Water Chestnuts.

ORIENTAL FRUIT FREEZE

one 3-ounce package cream cheese, at
  room temperature
¼ cup orange juice
one 8-ounce can crushed pineapple,
  drained

3 preserved kumquats, seeded and finely
  chopped
¼ cup chopped fresh dates
2 teaspoons chopped candied ginger
2 maraschino cherries, sliced

1. In a medium bowl, beat cream cheese until smooth. Gradually beat in orange juice.

2. Stir in drained pineapple, kumquats, dates and ginger. Spoon mixture into paper liners set in 2½-inch muffin pans. Garnish with sliced cherries. Freeze until firm, at least 1 hour.

CHINESE NOODLE NESTS

one 3-ounce package Oriental or
  cellophane noodles

vegetable oil for deep-fat frying

1. In a medium saucepan, cook noodles for about 3 minutes in boiling salted water to cover. Drain. Divide noodles into 4 portions. Press one portion at a time into a small strainer.

2. Use a fork to twirl noodles into a "nest." Pour oil to 3-inch depth in saucepan or deep-fat fryer; heat oil to 375° F. Fry each nest separately in hot fat until noodles crisp and brown. Drain on paper towels.

GREEN BEANS WITH WATER CHESTNUTS

1 pound fresh green beans, rinsed
2 tablespoons vegetable oil

½ teaspoon salt
½ cup chopped water chestnuts

1. Trim beans and cut on the diagonal into ¼-inch pieces. Heat oil in a frying pan or wok; add beans and stir-fry until crisp-tender, about 5 to 7 minutes.

2. To serve, toss beans with salt and water chestnuts.

ORANGE-CHICKEN DINNER

FRIED CHICKEN WITH
BROILED ORANGES*

SUCCOTASH WITH DILL

ROMAINE SALAD*

SHOOFLY GINGERBREAD*

Serves 4.

WORK PLAN: Purchase one family pack of fried chicken pieces from a franchise chicken store. Prepare Shoofly Gingerbread. Fifteen minutes before gingerbread is done, place fried chicken in large baking pan in oven to reheat. Then, make Romaine Salad. Cook one 16-ounce polybag frozen succotash according to label directions; drain and toss with 2 tablespoons butter or margarine and 1 teaspoon dill. Just as gingerbread and chicken are removed from oven, turn oven heat to broil and prepare Broiled Oranges. Place chicken on large warm platter and surround with oranges.

SHOOFLY GINGERBREAD

2 tablespoons butter or margarine	¼ cup sugar
¼ cup molasses	3 tablespoons flour
one 13½-ounce package gingerbread mix	2 tablespoons margarine

1. Preheat oven to 350° F. Put 2 tablespoons butter or margarine and ¼ cup molasses in bottom of 9-inch square baking pan. Place in oven to melt butter; swirl with a fork.

2. Mix gingerbread according to label directions. Pour batter into pan on top of molasses-butter mixture.

3. In a small bowl, mix sugar, flour and 2 tablespoons margarine until crumbly. Sprinkle evenly over batter. Bake 35 to 40 minutes, or until gingerbread is done. Cool on wire rack for 5 minutes.

4. Cut into squares and serve warm, either plain or with ice cream. *Serves about 6.*

ROMAINE SALAD

2 anchovy fillets	⅛ teaspoon garlic salt
2 tablespoons vinegar	⅛ teaspoon celery salt
¼ cup vegetable oil	1 small or ½ large head romaine lettuce,
⅛ teaspoon onion salt	rinsed and dried

1. Mash anchovy fillets in bottom of salad bowl. Blend in vinegar, oil, and onion, garlic and celery salt.

2. Tear romaine into chunky pieces and add to dressing in bowl. Just before serving, toss vigorously until all pieces are coated and glistening.

BROILED ORANGES

**2 large navel oranges, peeled and
     sectioned
2 teaspoons butter or margarine**

**4 teaspoons sugar
cinnamon**

1. Preheat broiler.

2. Place orange sections on broiler pan, dot with butter or margarine, then sprinkle with sugar and cinnamon.

3. Broil about 5 to 8 minutes or until bubbly and lightly browned. Serve hot with chicken.

For an alternate menu, try:

FRIED CHICKEN

HOT BISCUITS

SPICY TOMATOES AND LIMAS

GRAPEFRUIT, ORANGE AND
PINEAPPLE AMBROSIA

Use the same work plan, with the following changes:

Dessert
In large shallow serving bowl, arrange alternately 2 grapefruit, peeled and cut in ⅓-inch crosswise slices; 2 oranges, peeled and cut into ⅓-inch crosswise slices; and one 20-ounce can pineapple slices, drained (reserve juice). Pour the reserved pineapple juice over all; sprinkle heavily with one 3½-ounce can flaked coconut; chill.

Hot Biscuits
Prepare biscuits, using 2 cups prepared biscuit mix; bake while chicken is reheating.

Vegetables
In medium saucepan, combine one 32-ounce can whole peeled tomatoes, two 10-ounce packages frozen lima beans, 1 teaspoon salt and ½ teaspoon hot pepper sauce; simmer until beans are tender.

FISH DINNER

HERBED FISH BAKE*

FRENCH-FRIED POTATOES

ZUCCHINI AND TOMATOES*

FLAKY PEACH COBBLER*

Serves 6.

WORK PLAN: Purchase one franchise fish 'n' chips dinner consisting of 6 pieces coated fish and accompanying French fries. Prepare Flaky Peach Cobbler, then Herbed Fish Bake, setting fish on lower oven shelf to bake below dessert. Place French fries (chips) from fish dinner in a 13 x 9 x 2-inch baking dish, and warm beside fish. Prepare Zucchini and Tomatoes.

FLAKY PEACH COBBLER

one 21-ounce can peach pie filling
¼ cup water
¼ teaspoon cinnamon

one 8-ounce package refrigerator crescent rolls
1 tablespoon sugar

1. Preheat oven to 375° F. Pour pie filling into 9-inch round baking dish or cake pan. Rinse can with ¼ cup water; stir into filling. Sprinkle with cinnamon.

2. Separate rolls according to label directions. Arrange unbaked dough triangles on top of peach filling with points toward center of dish. Make a center vent by folding points back about ½ inch. Sprinkle sugar over triangles. Bake for 20 to 25 minutes, until top crust is golden brown. Serve warm with ice cream or whipped cream. *Serves 6 to 8.*

HERBED FISH BAKE

6 pieces cooked fish with batter or crumb coating
1 cup unflavored yogurt or sour cream
½ teaspoon crumbled tarragon

½ teaspoon crumbled thyme
½ teaspoon paprika
1 cup drained canned shrimp, or 1 cup peeled cooked shrimp

1. Arrange fish in lightly greased 12 x 8 x 2-inch baking dish.

2. Combine yogurt or sour cream, tarragon, thyme, paprika and shrimp; spoon down middle of baking dish over fish. Bake at 375° F for 10 to 15 minutes.

Note: To prevent curdling, bake only until sauce is very hot, but not bubbling.

ZUCCHINI AND TOMATOES

1 tablespoon vegetable oil
1 medium zucchini, thinly sliced
1 small onion, thinly sliced
1 firm tomato, thinly sliced

⅓ cup shredded American cheese
1 tablespoon chopped parsley
½ teaspoon salt
dash of pepper

1. Heat vegetable oil in large skillet over medium heat; add zucchini and onion and stir-fry for 4 or 5 minutes.

2. Stir in tomato, shredded cheese, parsley, salt and pepper. Cover, reduce heat to low and simmer for 4 minutes.

For an alternate menu, try:

HERBED FISH BAKE

FRENCH-FRIED POTATOES

PEAS AND CELERY SKILLET

APPLE WALNUT CRUMBLE

Use the same work plan, with the following changes:

Dessert
In 8 x 8 x 2-inch baking pan, place one 20-ounce can apple pie filling blended with 1 cup broken walnuts and 1 teaspoon grated lemon rind. Sprinkle over all 1 cup crushed coconut cookie crumbs; dot with 2 tablespoons butter or margarine. Bake at 375° F for 25 minutes.

Vegetables
In large skillet, sauté 2 cups thinly sliced celery in 3 tablespoons butter or margarine for 5 minutes; add two 10-ounce packages baby peas, slightly thawed, and 1½ teaspoons each salt, sugar and lemon rind. Cover and cook over low heat until peas are tender, about 5 to 7 minutes.

SHRIMP DINNER

FRENCH-FRIED SHRIMP

ZESTY RICE*

VEGETABLE SLAW*

WHOLE WHEAT MUFFINS*

STRAWBERRY MELBA*

Serves 4.

WORK PLAN: Purchase shrimp dinner for 4 from franchise fish restaurant. Prepare and chill peaches and strawberry sauce for Strawberry Melba; assemble just before dessert time. Prepare Vegetable Slaw; chill. Make Whole Wheat Muffins. About ten minutes before muffins are done, place shrimp dinner in 13 x 9 x 2-inch baking dish in oven to reheat. Meanwhile, prepare Zesty Rice.

STRAWBERRY MELBA

**2 fresh peaches, or 4 canned peach halves
one 10-ounce package frozen sliced
    strawberries, partially thawed**

1 pint vanilla ice cream

1. Peel and halve the fresh peaches, or drain the canned peach halves. Place a peach half hollow side up in each of 4 stemmed dessert dishes. Chill.

2. In electric blender, puree the partially thawed strawberries to a frosty slush; chill.

3. To serve, fill each peach half with a scoop of vanilla ice cream; top with chilled strawberry sauce.

Note: This dessert is equally good when frozen raspberries are used for the sauce.

VEGETABLE SLAW

**1 pint store-bought coleslaw
one 16-ounce can mixed vegetables,
    drained**

**1 teaspoon lemon juice
salt and pepper to taste
sour cream (optional)**

1. In a large bowl, combine coleslaw and mixed vegetables.

2. Add lemon juice, salt and pepper. Toss to mix.

3. Add 2 or 3 tablespoons sour cream, if you wish, for a creamier slaw.

WHOLE WHEAT MUFFINS

2 cups whole wheat flour
2 teaspoons baking powder
1 teaspoon soda
1 teaspoon salt

2 cups buttermilk
1 egg, beaten
¼ cup vegetable oil

1. Preheat oven to 400° F. Line twelve to sixteen 2½- to 3-inch muffin pans with paper liners, or grease muffin pans.

2. In a large mixing bowl, stir together flour, baking powder, soda and salt. Make a well in the middle; add buttermilk, egg and oil all at once.

3. Stir ingredients together, then beat until well mixed. Spoon batter into muffin pans, filling two-thirds full.

4. Bake 20 to 25 minutes until golden brown. *Makes 12 to 16 muffins.*

ZESTY RICE

2 tablespoons vegetable oil
1 cup coarsely chopped onion
1 cup chopped celery
one 16-ounce can tomato sauce

1 tablespoon horseradish
¼ teaspoon salt
generous dash of pepper
1½ cups quick-cooking rice

1. Heat vegetable oil in medium skillet or saucepan. Add onion and celery and sauté. Stir in tomato sauce.

2. Add horseradish, salt and pepper. Mix thoroughly and bring to boiling point. Stir in quick-cooking rice.

3. Cover and remove from heat; let stand about 5 minutes. Fluff with a fork before serving.

EnergySaving Tip: When you need a quick bread for a dinner that will be prepared with a minimum of heat, consider the following as alternatives to Whole Wheat Muffins:
• Store-bought plain or whole wheat muffins, sprinkled with grated sharp Cheddar cheese, broiled or heated in a toaster oven until the cheese melts.
• English muffins, split in half and spread with a mixture of ¼ cup butter or margarine, softened, ¼ cup grated Parmesan cheese and 1 small clove garlic, crushed; broil until crisp and bubbling.
• White, whole wheat or seedless rye bread (½-inch-thick slices), both sides spread with softened butter or margarine and sprinkled with sesame or caraway seeds. Press seeds into butter, then broil on both sides; cut into 1-inch fingers to serve.
• Thin slices of pumpernickel bread, sandwiched together with mixture of ¼ cup butter or margarine, softened, and ¼ cup crumbled blue cheese. Brush or spread outside of slices with a little additional butter or margarine; broil and cut sandwiches into three strips. Serve hot. These are excellent with salads.
• Pita or Middle-Eastern pocket breads, each cut into 6 triangles and each center spread with a little of a mixture of ¼ cup butter or margarine, softened, and ½ teaspoon each curry powder and cumin.

BUYING AND USING CHEESE

SOFT CHEESE

BOURSIN: A soft, triple crème cheese imported from France, gently flavored with herbs and a little garlic. Perfect to spread on fresh or crisp breads and crackers as an appetizer. Good as a dessert cheese with crisp apples and pears. Store, well wrapped, up to 2 weeks.

BRIE: Sold in thin wheels of varying diameters. The outer crust looks like fine, white, powdery pastry. When cut open, the inner, creamy center almost runs like thick cream. Smooth and mild in flavor, it is not to be confused with Camembert, which is much more pungent. Ideal for dessert with fresh fruit. When perfectly ripe, Brie keeps only 3 to 4 days.

CHEVRE CHEESE: Made of soft goats' milk curds and pressed into various small shapes (most often into cone shapes). The spelling of the name varies slightly according to region. Ideal as a snack on fresh bread; best for dessert with grapes, apricots or peaches. Store up to 3 to 4 weeks.

COTTAGE CHEESE: An American mild cheese; comes in either large or small curd, or else whipped until it is almost smooth (then it is called pot cheese). The simplest cheese to make, it is slightly acid and delicate in taste. Good for salads and with fruit. Check package for last date of sale.

CREAM CHEESE: American cream cheese has a high fat content, is mild, with a very delicate taste. It is best when used to carry other flavors, or as a spread on sandwiches or bagels, with the pungency of smoked salmon as a contrast. Cream cheese is an essential ingredient for cheesecake; a little goes well with crisp pears or apples. Store up to 4 weeks.

FETA CHEESE: A very large curd Greek cheese. It is white, very moist and preserved in brine. It has a sour, tangy flavor; best in Greek-style salads. It is also used in stuffed vegetables and pasta dishes. If stored in brine, the cheese keeps up to 4 weeks; otherwise, 1 week.

NEUFCHATEL CHEESE: One of the most famous cream cheeses of Normandy; sold in various shapes. It has more flavor than American cream cheese. Crema Danica is also of the same family with a different but still mild flavor. Good for appetizers and as part of a fruit and cheese board. Store up to 10 days.

RICOTTA: A thick creamed cottage cheese; somewhat thicker, sweeter and smoother than American cottage cheese. Use to fill many differently shaped pastas or tossed into noodles; it can also be sweetened with sugar and chocolate for a dessert. Check container for last date of sale.

SEMISOFT CHEESE

BEL PAESE: Of Italian origin, now made also in the United States; semisoft in texture, mild and creamy in flavor. It must be perfectly ripe and served at room temperature; good as an appetizer with prosciutto, or in a salad, or with grapes or pineapple for dessert. Store up to 10 days.

BRICK: A cheese that originated in the United States; it can be soft to firm in texture and buttery mild to sharp in flavor, depending on the age of the cheese. Less aged cheese, an even cream color with little rind, is preferred. Best served as a snack or in sandwiches, especially with rye or pumpernickel bread. Store up to 1 month.

COLBY: A cheese that originated in the United States, made in Wisconsin and Vermont. A mild-flavored, granular, open-textured cheese, similar to soft Cheddar in appearance and taste. Good for snacks and sandwiches and with crisp apples for dessert. Store up to 1 month.

DANBO: A Danish cheese; mild, very pliable and semisoft in texture, with numerous small holes. At room temperature, it has an even, shiny appearance throughout. Its flavor is mild and sweet; often flavored with caraway. Samsoe cheese, often called Danish Swiss, is very similar. Good for snacks and sandwiches. Store up to 4 weeks.

FONTINA: From the Alp region in the northern part of Italy, it has a thin, pale brown-yellow rind and a creamy firm interior that becomes slightly buttery at room temperature. Its flavor is a mixture of Swiss and Port du Salut. A good melting cheese for fondue, excellent when served with grapes, peaches, apricots. Store up to 2 to 3 weeks.

MONTEREY JACK: A California cheese in origin, often thought to have first been made by the Spanish missions. Shaped like a brick with almost no rind, it is cured only 3 to 6 weeks; it has high moisture content, is pale white-yellow in color, slightly salty in taste. Best for appetizers, cooking and sandwiches. Store up to 4 weeks.

MOZZARELLA: Italian in origin, a lightly cooked cheese which was originally made from buffalo's milk, now made from cows' milk. White, soft and rindless, it has a slightly salty, acid flavor. Best used as a topping for pizza, as a stuffing for pasta. Store up to 2 weeks.

MUENSTER: Alsace-German in origin, it is brick-shaped with a thin, bright red skin. It has a semisoft interior, a little like Danbo, but without the shiny quality. It has a slightly salty, tangy flavor and a distinctive aroma; it is sometimes flavored with caraway. Best used as an appetizer, for sandwiches, or with crisp firm fruit for dessert. Store up to 3 to 4 weeks.

FIRM CHEESE

DANISH BLUE: A Danish cheese. Very white, with distinctive blue mottling; very sharp salty flavor, butter-firm in texture; strong sharp aroma. Use in salads; serve with chilled apples. Store up to 4 to 6 weeks.

CHEDDAR: Originally made in England; now made in the United States, usually Wisconsin, New York and Vermont. Made in wheel shapes with a characteristic black rind, its interior is pale cream-orange. A moist cheese, firm enough to slice; a mild flavor after 6 months' aging, a deeper, pungent, sharper flavor afterwards. Store up to 6 weeks.

CHESHIRE: English in origin, its flavor and texture cannot be duplicated; moister and crumblier than Cheddar, the distinctive flavor comes from buttermilk and the salt grass of Cheshire. Perfect as an appetizer with raw vegetables, excellent for grilled sandwiches. Store from 4 to 6 weeks.

GORGONZOLA: A blue cheese, Italian in origin (green in its veining, rather than blue); firm, but the most buttery of veined cheese. It has greater fat content than Roquefort, is moister than Stilton, and has the most pungent aroma of all blue cheese. Store up to 6 months, depending on preferred ripeness.

GOUDA: Traditional Dutch cheese, made from whole milk, shaped into flat wheel with yellow rind. Smooth and mellow, with mild flavor. Best used for snacks or with juicy soft berries. Do not use for cooking. Store up to 2 months.

GRUYERE: A Swiss cheese, smaller in size and with smaller holes than Emmentaler, creamier in texture with a sharp nutty flavor. Ideal for appetizers, sandwiches, cooking, and as an accompaniment to fruit. Store up to 6 weeks.

HAVARTI: Danish in origin; used to be called Danish Tilsit. Sold in blocks; deep yellow rind; the interior is pale butter color with irregular holes. It has a mild but sour-sharp flavor. Good for appetizers and sandwiches. Store up to 4 weeks.

ROQUEFORT: French in origin, and the most important blue cheese from France; made from sheep's milk and ripened in caves in the Pyrenees. It has a pungent taste and aroma. Serve with crisp bread or with perfectly ripe pears. Store up to 6 months, depending on ripeness.

VERY HARD CHEESE

ASIAGO: Once made from sheep's milk in Sicily, now made from cows' milk in Michigan and Wisconsin. When not cured more than 60 days, can be served as a table cheese. When aged 6 months or more, it is a superior grating cheese; use in hot pasta or for toppings. Store up to 6 months.

CACIOCAVALLO: Italian, made of cows' milk; very much like provolone in shape and appearance. It has a salty, smoke flavor. Best used as a cooking cheese. Store up to 6 months.

EMMENTALER: Swiss in origin, white-cream in color; although hard in texture, its flavor is nutty and sweet. Ideal for grating and for use in fondues. Store up to 2 to 3 months.

PARMESAN: Italian in origin; a very, very hard cheese with a distinctive salty flavor; must be grated very finely before using; toss with hot pasta or use as a topping. Genuine Parmesan is aged 2 to 3 years; store indefinitely.

PECORINO: Italian in origin; a very hard cheese made from sheep's milk, though now imitated in the United States, Canada and Australia with cows' milk. Very pungent in taste and aroma; finely grate before using for cooking in pasta. Store indefintely.

PROVOLONE: Italian in origin, made from the milk of buffalo, sheep or cows. It has a sharp, hot, salty flavor. It can be eaten very fresh as a table cheese, with salad or with fruit; if aged, it is best grated and used for cooking. It keeps indefinitely, if stored unopened in its traditional thick wax rind.

ROMANO: An alternative to Parmesan cheese; if used fresh, it can be served as a table cheese; after one year, it ages to a grating-cooking cheese. Store indefinitely.

SAPSAGO: Swiss in origin; a very hard, green, small, cone-shaped cheese. Very pungent because it is made from sour milk, buttermilk and whey, and flavored with dried aromatic clover. It is used, finely grated, as a table condiment; store indefinitely.

INDEX